GW00702802

Test

Business Vocabulary

Intermediate

Kenna Bourke
and Amanda Maris

OXFORD

UNIVERSITY PRESS

OXFORD
UNIVERSITY PRESS

Great Clarendon Street, Oxford OX2 6DP

Oxford University Press is a department of the University of Oxford.
It furthers the University's objective of excellence in research, scholarship,
and education by publishing worldwide in

Oxford New York

Auckland Cape Town Dar es Salaam Hong Kong Karachi
Kuala Lumpur Madrid Melbourne Mexico City Nairobi
New Delhi Shanghai Taipei Toronto

With offices in

Argentina Austria Brazil Chile Czech Republic France Greece
Guatemala Hungary Italy Japan Poland Portugal Singapore
South Korea Switzerland Thailand Turkey Ukraine Vietnam

OXFORD and OXFORD ENGLISH are registered trade marks of
Oxford University Press in the UK and in certain other countries

ISBN-13: 978 0 19 439205 1
ISBN-10: 0 19 439205 8

Printed in Spain by Unigraf S.L.

Contents

How to use *Test it, Fix it*   **4**

Jobs   6

Departments   10

Office equipment   14

The internet   18

Emailing   22

Formal letters   26

Job applications   30

Promotion and unemployment   34

Working conditions   38

Pay and benefits   42

Giving opinions   46

Meetings   50

Numbers and figures   54

The phone   58

Marketing   62

Time   66

Business travel   70

Cultural matters   74

Presentations   78

Conferences   82

British and American English   **86**

Useful information   **88**

How to use *Test it, Fix it*

Test it, Fix it is a series of books designed to help you identify any problems you may have in English, and to fix the problems. Each *Test it, Fix it* book has twenty tests which concentrate on mistakes commonly made by learners.

Test it, Fix it has an unusual format. You start at the **first** page of each unit, then go to the **third** page, then to the **second** page. Here's how it works:

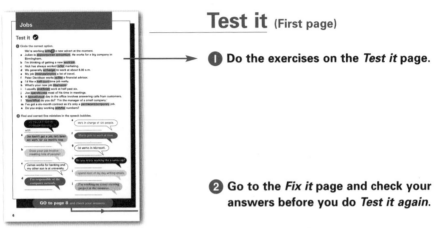

Test it (First page)

① Do the exercises on the *Test it* page.

② Go to the *Fix it* page and check your answers before you do *Test it again*.

Fix it (Third page)

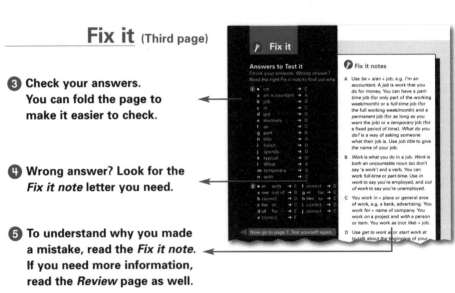

③ Check your answers. You can fold the page to make it easier to check.

④ Wrong answer? Look for the *Fix it note* letter you need.

⑤ To understand why you made a mistake, read the *Fix it note*. If you need more information, read the *Review* page as well.

⑥ Now go back to the second page and do *Test it again*.

Test it again (Second page)

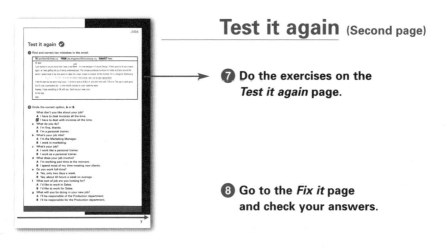

7 Do the exercises on the *Test it again* page.

8 Go to the *Fix it* page and check your answers.

Fix it (Third page)

9 Check your answers.

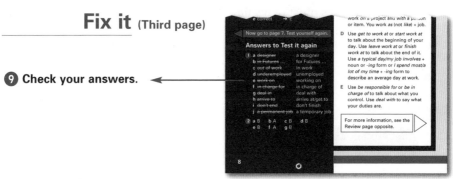

Review (Fourth page)

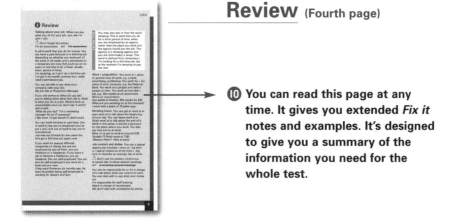

10 You can read this page at any time. It gives you extended *Fix it* notes and examples. It's designed to give you a summary of the information you need for the whole test.

5

Jobs

Test it ✔

❶ Circle the correct option.

We're working with/**on** a new advert at the moment.

a Julian is accountant/**an accountant**. He works for a big company in Birmingham.

b I'm thinking of getting a new work/**job**.

c Nick has always worked **in**/for marketing.

d We generally **arrive**/get to work at about 8.00 a.m.

e My job **involves**/implies a lot of travel.

f Peter Davidson works **as**/like a financial advisor.

g I'd like a **half**-/part-time job really.

h What's your new job **title**/name?

i I usually **end**/finish work at half past six.

j Joe **spends**/uses most of his time in meetings.

k A **typical**/usual day in the office involves answering calls from customers.

l 'How/**What** do you do?' 'I'm the manager of a small company.'

m I've got a six-month contract so it's only a permanent/**temporary** job.

n Do you enjoy working **with**/for numbers?

❷ Find and correct five mistakes in the speech bubbles.

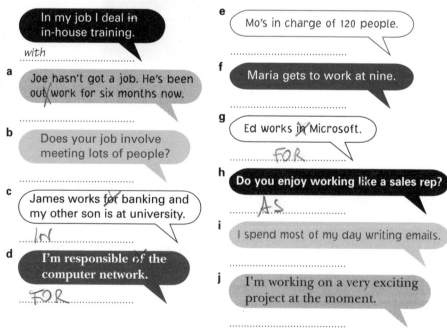

In my job I deal ~~in~~ in-house training.
with

a Joe hasn't got a job. He's been out/work for six months now.

b Does your job involve meeting lots of people?

c James works for/ banking and my other son is at university.
IN

d I'm responsible of the computer network.
FOR

e Mo's in charge of 120 people.

f Maria gets to work at nine.

g Ed works in/Microsoft.
FOR

h Do you enjoy working like a sales rep?
AS

i I spend most of my day writing emails.

j I'm working on a very exciting project at the moment.

GO to page 8 and check your answers.

Test it again ✔

1 **Find and correct ten mistakes in the email.**

TO Jane.Beach@citiweb.org **FROM** jake.wrigglestock@futuresdesign.org **SUBJECT** News
Hi Jane I just wanted to let you know that I have a new ~~work~~ *job* – I'm now designer ~~in~~ *in* Futures Design. It feels good to be ~~out of~~ work again, as I was getting fed up of being ~~underemployed~~. The company produces furniture for hotels and bars around the world. I spend most of my time ~~work~~ on ideas for a chain of bars in London. At the moment, I'm in charge ~~for~~ *of* developing some interesting but comfortable chairs! I also deal ~~in~~ *with* the clients, who can be very demanding! I like the team but we work long hours – I arrive to work at 8.00 a.m. and don't ~~end~~ *finish* until 7.00 p.m. The pay is quite good, but it's only a ~~permanent~~ *temporary* job – a nine-month contract to cover maternity leave. Anyway, I hope everything is OK with you. Send me your news soon. All the best Jake

(handwritten annotations: job, for, in, of, with, temporary, finish, arrive at, or)

2 **Circle the correct option, A or B.**

What don't you like about your job?
  A I have to deal invoices all the time.
  (B) I have to deal with invoices all the time.

a What do you do?
  A I'm fine, thanks.
  (B) I'm a personal trainer.

b What's your job title?
  (A) I'm the Marketing Manager.
  B I work in marketing.

c What's your job?
  A I work like a personal trainer.
  (B) I work as a personal trainer.

d What does your job involve?
  A I'm working part-time at the moment.
  (B) I spend most of my time meeting new clients.

e Do you work full-time?
  A Yes, only two days a week.
  (B) Yes, about 40 hours a week on average.

f What sort of job are you looking for?
  (A) I'd like to work in Sales.
  B I'd like to work for Sales.

g What will you be doing in your new job?
  A I'll be responsible of the Production department.
  (B) I'll be responsible for the Production department.

Fix it

Answers to Test it

Check your answers. Wrong answer? Read the right Fix it note to find out why.

1	•	on	→	C
	a	an accountant	→	A
	b	job	→	B
	c	in	→	C
	d	get	→	D
	e	involves	→	D
	f	as	→	C
	g	part-	→	A
	h	title	→	A
	i	finish	→	D
	j	spends	→	D
	k	typical	→	D
	l	What	→	A
	m	temporary	→	A
	n	with	→	C

2	•	~~in~~ with	→	E	f	correct	→	D
	a	~~out~~ out of	→	B	g	~~in~~ for	→	C
	b	correct	→	D	h	~~like~~ as	→	C
	c	~~for~~ in	→	C	i	correct	→	D
	d	~~of~~ for	→	E	j	correct	→	C
	e	correct	→	E				

Now go to page 7. Test yourself again.

Answers to Test it again

1	a	~~designer~~	a designer
	b	~~in Futures ...~~	for Futures ...
	c	~~out of work~~	in work
	d	~~underemployed~~	unemployed
	e	~~work on~~	working on
	f	~~in charge for~~	in charge of
	g	~~deal in~~	deal with
	h	~~arrive to~~	arrive at/get to
	i	~~don't end~~	don't finish
	j	~~a permanent job~~	a temporary job

2	a B	b A	c B	d B
	e B	f A	g B	

Fix it notes

A Use *be* + *a/an* + job, e.g. *I'm an accountant.* A *job* is work that you do for money. You can have a *part-time* job (for only part of the working week/month) or a *full-time* job (for the full working week/month) and a *permanent* job (for as long as you want the job) or a *temporary* job (for a fixed period of time). *What do you do?* is a way of asking someone what their job is. Use *job title* to give the name of your job.

B *Work* is what you do in a job. *Work* is both an uncountable noun (so don't say 'a work') and a verb. You can work *full-time* or *part-time*. Use *in work* to say you're employed, and *out of work* to say you're unemployed.

C You work *in* + place or general area of work, e.g. a bank, advertising. You work *for* + name of company. You work *on* a project and *with* a person or item. You work *as* (not *like*) + job.

D Use *get to work at* or *start work at* to talk about the beginning of your day. Use *leave work at* or *finish work at* to talk about the end of it. Use *a typical day/my job involves* + noun or *-ing* form or *I spend most/a lot of my time* + *-ing* form to describe an average day at work.

E Use *be responsible for* or *be in charge of* to talk about what you control. Use *deal with* to say what your duties are.

For more information, see the Review page opposite.

ℹ Review

Talking about your job When you say what you do for your job, you use *I'm a/an* + Job.

⚠ Don't forget the article.
I'm an accountant. NOT ~~I'm accountant.~~

A *job* is work that you do for money. You can have a *part-time* job or a *full-time* job depending on whether you work part of the week or all week, and a *permanent* or a *temporary* job (one that could go on for years or one that is for a fixed, usually short, period of time).
I'm studying, so I can't do a full-time job.
I've got a six-month contract but I really need a permanent job.

You use *job title* to say what your company calls your job.
My job title is Production Manager.

If you ask someone *What do you do?*, you're asking them what their job is. *Work* is what you do in a job. *Work* is both an uncountable noun (so don't say 'a work') and a verb.
'What do you do?' 'I'm a marketing manager for an IT company.'
I like work. I'd get bored if I didn't work.

You can *work full-time* or *part-time*. Use *in work* to say you're employed (you've got a job), and *out of work* to say you're unemployed.
Joe was out of work for two years but he works full-time again now.

If you work for several different companies or clients, but are not employed by any of them, you are *freelance* or a *freelancer*. If you leave a job to become a freelancer, you *go freelance*. You are *self-employed*. You can also be self-employed if you work for a business you own.
Craig went freelance six months ago. He says he prefers being self-employed to working for Spears and Son.

EXTRA TIPS

You may also see or hear the word *temping*. This is work that you do for a short period of time, when you are employed by an agency rather than the place you work and the agency found you the job. The agency is a *temping agency* and you are (informally) a *temp*. (The word is derived from *temporary*.)
I'm looking for a full-time job, but at the moment I'm temping to pay the rent.

Work + preposition You work *in* + place or general area of work, e.g. a bank, advertising, publishing. You work *for* + the name of your company, e.g. the National Bank. You work *on* a project and *with* a person or item. You work *as* (not *like*) + job, e.g. *She works as an accountant.* (She's an accountant.)
Sue works in finance. She works for SSI.
What are you working on at the moment?
I work with a team of 15 sales reps.

Working hours You use *get to work at* or *start work at* to talk about the beginning of your day. You use *leave work at* or *finish work at* to talk about the end of it. *Work* in this sense is almost a synonym for the place where you work. You also say that you're *at work*.
Most of us get to work at around 8.30.
Tonight I'll finish work at 7.00.
'Where's Peter?' 'He's at work.'

Job content and duties You use *a typical day/my job involves* + noun or *-ing* form or *I spend most/a lot of my time* + *-ing* form to describe an average day at work.

⚠ Don't use the present continuous.
A typical day involves several meetings.
NOT ~~is involving several meetings~~

You use *be responsible for* or *be in charge of* to talk about what you control at work. You use *deal with* to say what your duties are.
I'm responsible for staff training.
Mae's in charge of recruitment.
We don't deal with complaints by phone.

Departments

Test it ✅

1 Circle the correct option.

If you wish to complain, please contact (Customer)/Consumer Services.

a HR stands for Human Relations/(Resources).
b IT is short for Information Techniques/(Technology).
c (Positive)/Public Relations is often known as PR.
d R&D stands for Research and (Development)/Designs.
e My department is quite small – just three designers and our line (manager)/director.
f In my department we (liaise)/liaison very closely with Sales.
g Communication in the department isn't very good – we need to try a (team-building)/team-making exercise.
h My boss dictates/(delegates) a lot of the work to the rest of the department.
i The staff (turnover)/turnaround is very high in our department – people leave all the time.
j I don't deal with invoices – talk to Dave in (Finance)/Financial.

2 Match speakers **a–j** to departments **1–10**.

a I spend most of my day updating software.
b I've just written an advert for new sales staff.
c I look after all the contracts.
d We develop new products and services.
e We deal with people's complaints.
f I control the budgets.
g Our campaign brought us ten new customers.
h I've just updated the schedule for the new model.
i We hope this campaign will improve our image.
j We have to get the new designs into the shops by the first of December.

1 Legal
2 Customer Services
3 Production
4 HR
5 IT
6 R&D
7 Distribution
8 PR
9 Finance
10 Sales and Marketing

a 5
b 4
c 1
d 6
e 2
f 9
g 10
h 3
i 8
j 7

GO to page 12 and check your answers.

Test it again ✔

1 **Choose the correct words to complete the dialogue.**

turnover   *Marketing*   *team-building*   ~~liaison~~   ~~IT~~
Finance   *line manager*   *HR*   *delegates*

EMMA OK, Vicky, so why do you want to leave .....IT....................? I thought you
were happy working on the computer network.

VICKY Well, I find the work a bit boring and I don't get on with my
a .... very well. He **b** .... all the difficult tasks to me
and I'm fed up with it. And the **c** .... with other departments is
bad – they all think we can't talk about anything but computers. I like
working with people so that's why I want to join **d** ....

EMMA Yes, but there aren't any jobs there at the moment. They have the lowest
staff **e** .... in the whole company. But you're good with
numbers – why don't you apply for the job in **f** ....?

VICKY No way! I don't want to become an accountant! I want to try something
more creative.

EMMA Well, they need someone in **g** .... to promote our new
personal organizer.

VICKY That sounds interesting. They do lots of fun **h** .... exercises,
don't they?

2 **Should these people stay or move to another department?**

Kate from HR: 'I love working with people and making sure
they're happy at work.'   .....stay.........

a Jo from Customer Services: 'I hate talking to customers on
the phone.'   ....

b Amy from Sales: 'My team always meets its targets.'   ....

c Mike from Production: 'I forgot to give the factory manager
the revised schedule.'   ....

d Leo from R&D: 'It's really hard to come up with new ideas –
I just copy what other companies do.'   ....

e Diane from Distribution: 'It's great to see all our products
in the right place at just the right time.'   ....

f Sarah from Legal: 'I didn't get the supplier to sign the
contract, so we lost thousands of dollars.'   ....

g Harry from PR: 'We're the best-loved food company in this
country and I want to keep it that way.'   ....

h Des from IT: 'I tested the network and the whole system
shut down for three days.'   ....

🔧 Fix it

Answers to Test it

Check your answers. Wrong answer?
Read the right Fix it note to find out why.

1. ● Customer → G
   a Resources → A
   b Technology → A
   c Public → A
   d Development → A
   e manager → B
   f liaise → C
   g team-building → C
   h delegates → B
   i turnover → D
   j Finance → E

2. a 5 → A   f 9 → E
   b 4 → A   g 10 → G
   c 1 → E   h 3 → F
   d 6 → A   i 8 → A
   e 2 → G   j 7 → F

Now go to page 11. Test yourself again.

Answers to Test it again

1. a line manager
   b delegates
   c liaison
   d HR
   e turnover
   f Finance
   g Marketing
   h team-building

2. a move
   b stay
   c move
   d move
   e stay
   f move
   g stay
   h move

🔧 Fix it notes

A   HR (Human Resources) deals with recruitment and staff problems; IT (Information Technology) deals with computers and technical support; PR (Public Relations) deals with an organization's image; R&D (Research and Development) deals with developing new ideas/products.

B   Your line manager is the person in charge of your work. You delegate when you give a task/responsibility to someone more junior.

C   Use liaise when you talk to another person/department in order to work more effectively. Organizations sometimes use team-building exercises/activities to help improve communication and performance.

D   Use staff turnover to talk about the rate at which staff leave an organization and new people arrive.

E   The Legal department deals with all aspects of the law that relate to an organization; the Finance department deals with all aspects of money.

F   Production deals with the making of products that can be sold; Distribution deals with getting things to customers.

G   Sales and Marketing deals with creating markets and selling products; Customer Services deals with customers' questions and complaints.

For more information, see the Review page opposite. ▷

ℹ Review

Abbreviations You sometimes use abbreviations to refer to departments. *HR (Human Resources)* deals with recruitment and staff problems. HR is called *Personnel* in some organizations.
Any staff problems are dealt with by our Personnel department.

IT (Information Technology) deals with computers and technical support.
Ask IT to check that your computer is linked to the network.

PR (Public Relations) deals with an organization's image outside the company.
The PR department needs to get the public to trust the company.

R&D (Research and Development) deals with developing new ideas and products.
R&D are looking at new ways of packaging food.

Law and finance The *Legal* department deals with all aspects of the law that relate to an organization. The *Finance* department deals with all aspects of money.
A revised contract will be sent to you from our Legal department.
You can claim your expenses from the Finance department.

Production and distribution The *Production* department deals with all aspects of the making of things so that they can be sold. The *Distribution* department deals with all aspects of getting things to a customer.
Please check with Production which factory we are using.
Distribution will need to coordinate delivery to the supermarkets.

Sales and marketing The *Sales* and *Marketing* departments deal with all aspects of creating markets and selling products. In many organizations the two departments are combined. The *Customer Services* department deals with customers' questions and complaints.
The sales figures are bad – we need a new campaign from Sales and Marketing.
See Customer Services with all queries.

Working with colleagues You use *line manager* to talk about the person who is in charge of the work you do. More informally, this person is your *boss*. You use the verb *delegate* when you give a task/responsibility to someone junior.
How much work does your line manager delegate to you?
I'm lucky to have such an understanding boss.

Use *liaise* when you talk to another person/department in order to work more effectively. The noun is *liaison*. Organizations sometimes use *team-building exercises/activities* to help improve communication and performance.
All departments will need to liaise on this project.
We need to improve liaison with our key clients.
We went mountain-climbing as a team-building exercise.

Structuring You use *staff turnover* to talk about the rate at which staff leave an organization and new people arrive.
Why is the turnover so high in the IT department?

EXTRA TIPS

You talk about people working at different *levels* (not *ranks*): more senior people are *higher level*; more junior people are *lower level*; people who do the same job as you, or who are neither more senior nor more junior, are *at/on the same level.*
I'm afraid I can't help you – you'll need to speak to someone at a higher level.

The person in charge of each department is usually called the *head*, e.g. *head of Sales*. At senior levels they may be called *director* instead/as well.
Oli Sharf is head of Customer Services, but he's applied to become the director of Sales and Marketing.

Office equipment

Test it ✔

1 Choose the correct words to complete the sentences.

digital   PC   mouse   laptop   drive   ~~speakers~~
webcam   internet   screen   keyboard   PDA

You can hear sound through the *speakers* on your computer.
a You type on a *keyboard* .
b A small computer you use when travelling is called a *laptop* .
c You use a *webcam* connected to a computer to produce images that you can see on a website.
d When you're using a computer, you look at the *screen* .
e Cameras you use with computers are *digitals* .
f A very small computer that you can hold in your hand is sometimes called a *PDA* .
g You can get information by surfing the *Internet* .
h You click with a *mouse* .
i A larger computer you use in the office is often called a *PC* .
j You receive information from a disk through the CD or DVD *drive* .

2 Circle the correct option.

I use my (palmtop)/handtop on the bus to work.
a I need to take/(make) a phone call to a colleague.
b You can make/(take) photos on a mobile now.
c Could you switch the webcam on/(off)? It's using a lot of memory.
d Those speakers are loud! Turn the volume up/(down) on your computer.
e Where's the scanner/(printer)? I need to send out a copy of this document by post.
f Oh no, the photocopier/(scanner) isn't working. I wanted to copy this graph on to the computer and add it to my report.
g The screen is very dark. Can you switch/(turn) up the brightness?
h Seventeen people were fired for (surfing)/sailing the internet at work.

GO to page 16 and check your answers.

Test it again ✓

1 Solve the clues to complete the crossword.

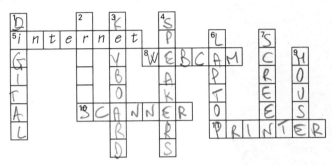

Across

5 A network of computers in different parts of the world. (8)

8 You use this to see the person you're emailing. (6)

10 You use this to put text/images into digital form. (7)

11 You use this to get hard copy of a document. (7)

Down

1 An adjective to describe things which use information stored as numbers. (7)

2 DVD and CD, for example. (6)

3 The part of a computer you type on. (8)

4 You use these to listen to sounds and music on your computer. (8)

6 A computer you carry around with you and can use anywhere. (6)

7 You can see the words you type on it. (6)

9 A small thing you click when you're using a computer. (5)

2 Find and correct five mistakes in the sentences.

This program sends and ~~takes~~ emails.   *receives*

a I ~~made~~ these photos on my new digital camera!   TAKE

b ~~Switch~~ the volume up – I can't hear it!   TURN

c There's something wrong with my key~~board~~ – I can't click on a document.   MOUSE

d My screen has gone blank. I can't see the text.

e Don't forget to turn the webcam off.

f How do I turn the volume down on this laptop?

g I'm going on a business trip but I'm taking my ~~PC~~ with me.   LAPTOP

h I need to ~~do~~ a call to the office. Can I borrow your mobile?   MAKE

i This laptop's very small. It doesn't have a DVD drive.

j Wait a second. I'm just printing this report.

🔧 Fix it

Answers to Test it

Check your answers. Wrong answer?
Read the right Fix it note to find out why.

1 • speakers → C
  a keyboard → C
  b laptop → A
  c webcam → C
  d screen → C
  e digital → B
  f PDA → A
  g internet → B
  h mouse → C
  i PC → A
  j drive → C

2 • palmtop → A
  a make → E
  b take → E
  c off → F
  d down → F
  e printer → D
  f scanner → D
  g turn → F
  h surfing → E

Now go to page 15. Test yourself again.

Answers to Test it again

1

2 The incorrect sentences are:
  a ~~made~~   took
  b ~~Switch~~   Turn
  c ~~keyboard~~   mouse
  g ~~PC~~   laptop/PDA
  h ~~do~~   make

🔧 Fix it notes

A Computers can be called *PCs* (Personal Computer) or *laptops*. You can also have a hand-held computer, sometimes called a *PDA* (Personal Digital Assistant) or a *palmtop*. Use *PC* for home or office computers. You can carry laptops and PDAs.

B Use *digital* to describe equipment that stores information as numbers or electronic signals, e.g. *digital camera, recording*. Use *the internet* to talk about the network of computers across the world that can exchange information; use the *world wide web* to talk about the information that is stored on these computers.

C The main parts of a computer are the *screen* (which you look at), the *keyboard* (for typing) and the *mouse* (for clicking etc.). Other features include the *CD/DVD drives* which let you access information on a disk, *speakers* which send out sound, and a *webcam* that can produce images which can be seen on a website.

D A *printer* gives you a hard (paper) copy of a document; a *scanner* puts text/images into digital form. A *photocopier* copies documents.

E You *take* (not *make*) a photo. You *make* a phone call. You *surf* the internet.

F You *switch* or *turn* computers, phones, cameras, etc. *on* and *off* but you *turn* (not *switch*) the volume *up* and *down*.

For more information, see the Review page opposite. ▷

ⓘ Review

Computers There are several different types of computer. The word you choose to describe them usually depends on their size. A *PC* (Personal Computer) is a computer which you use at home or in an office. It usually has four separate parts: the computer itself, the screen, the mouse and the keyboard. The *screen* or *monitor* is the thing you look at, the *keyboard* is for typing, and the *mouse* is for clicking. PCs are also sometimes called *desktop computers* or just *desktops*.
We ordered 200 new PCs, but we didn't know that monitors weren't included in the price.

A *laptop* is a smaller computer. It's called a laptop because it fits on your lap (your knees). It doesn't usually have a separate keyboard and screen. You often use a laptop when you need to move around because it's easy to carry. You can also have a *hand-held computer* called a *PDA* (Personal Digital Assistant) or *palmtop*. This is a very small computer that fits in your hand.
When I'm away on long trips, I take a laptop. On shorter trips, I use my PDA.

Other features on a computer include the *CD/DVD drives* which let you access information on a disk, *speakers* which send out sound, and a *webcam* that can produce images which can be seen on a website.
There's something wrong with these speakers. I can't hear a thing!
If you want to see exactly what goes on at BuildBlox, log on to their website and watch the webcam.

Other office equipment Other equipment includes a *printer* which gives you a hard (paper) copy of a document and a *scanner* which puts text/images into digital form. A *photocopier* makes copies of documents.
Once you've scanned the image, send it to the printer to get a hard copy of it.

You use the word *digital* to describe equipment that stores information as numbers or electronic signals, e.g. *digital camera, recording.*
The sound quality is excellent on this because it's a digital recording.

The internet People often refer to *the internet* and *the world wide web* to mean the same thing, but there is a difference. You use *the internet* (often just called *the net*) to talk about the network of computers across the world that can exchange information; you use *the world wide web* to talk about the information that is stored on these computers.
Remember it's always *the internet* (not *internet*).
I'll look it up on the internet.
NOT *on internet*

Verbs and prepositions You *take* (not *make*) a photo. You *surf* the internet. You *make* a phone call.
Have you taken the photos for the new project?
He's surfing the net.
I need to make a call.

You *switch* or *turn* computers, phones, cameras etc. *on* and *off* but you *turn* (not *switch*) the volume *up* and *down.*
How do I switch this mobile on?
Can you turn the volume down?

EXTRA TIPS
A *memory stick* is a small device that plugs into a computer, for storing information and transferring information between computers.
This memory stick stores 1GB of information, and it's smaller than my little finger.

The internet

Test it ✔

1 Answer the questions. Circle the correct option.

Do you …

(go to), come to or go at a web page?
a push, press or (click) on a link?
b write, (enter) or provide your password?
c enclose, connect or (attach) a document?
d (start up), begin or commence a computer?
e end, finish or (shut down) a computer?
f read, (surf) or watch the internet?
g transmit, (send) or post an email?
h attach, (connect) or join to the internet?
i (save), conserve or (keep) a document?
j erase, destroy or (delete) a document?

2 Put the words under the correct verbs. Some words may go under two verbs.

| your computer | the internet | an email | a document |
| a photo | a link | a program | a web page |

search	scan	download	send	surf
the internet	A photo	a photo	an email	the internet
	a document	a program	a document	

3 Complete the sentences with a suitable preposition.

Make sure you log ...out......... of your internet bank account.
a Click ...on...... 'save as' to save the document.
b Scroll ...up...... to see the top of the document.
c Scroll ...down... to see the end of the document.
d Connect ...to........ the internet and open your browser.
e Start ...up...... your computer and enter your password.
f Don't forget to shut down... your computer before you leave.
g Go ...to......... the homepage of the company's website.
h Before you print a document, switch the printer ...on...... .
i Don't switch .... your computer before shutting it down.
j You need to enter a password to log ...on..... and read your mail.

GO to page 20 and check your answers.

Test it again ✅

1 Solve the clues to complete the crossword.

Across

2 I often ___ the net when I need facts and figures. (4)

6 Some web pages take ages to ___. (8)

7 If you ___ down the page, you'll see a photo of the property. (6)

8 If you want to keep your document, you need to ___ it. (4)

9 I never ___ my emails so I have thousands of them! (6)

10 To find out more, ___ to www.oup.com. (2)

11 Don't forget to ___ a photo next time you send me an email. (6)

Down

1 Can you ___ me a link to your website? (4)

2 I really need to ___ my computer for viruses. (4)

3 I've got problems. I can't ___ to the internet today. (7)

4 You should ___ out of your account before leaving the website. (3)

5 ___ on the Start button, then open the program. (5)

7 I need to know how much flights to Osaka are, so I'll ___ the web. (6)

9 I'm going home. Can you shut ___ the computer for me? (4)

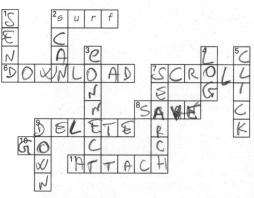

Crossword answers shown: 2 across SURF; 1 down SEND; 2 down SCAN; 3 down CONNECT; 6 across DOWNLOAD; 7 across SCROLL; 4 down LOG; 5 down CLICK; 8 across SAVE; 9 across DELETE; 10 across GO; 11 across ATTACH

2 Find and correct the mistakes in the email.

TO Robert.Parkin@Persona.org **FROM** PatrickClover@yerhagh.com **SUBJECT** Documents attached

Hi Bob

I hope you ~~took~~ [got/received] the photo I ~~posted~~ [sent] you ~~in~~ [by] an email yesterday. I'm ~~enclosing~~ [attaching] two documents ~~with~~ [to] this email.
If you ~~scroll into~~ [search/look] the first document, you'll find a link. ~~Press~~ [click] on the link to ~~surf~~ [download/go to] the web page. When you get there, you
need to ~~write~~ [type/enter] a password. Then you can ~~erase~~ [delete] document 1. Please ~~put away~~ [save] document 2 on your computer.
I'm having problems ~~attaching~~ [connecting] to the internet today so don't be surprised if you don't hear from me again. It's a pity. I love
~~watching~~ [surfing] the internet, as you know. (scroll/look down)

Bye for now

Patrick

Answers to Test it

Check your answers. Wrong answer?
Read the right Fix it note to find out why.

1 • go to   → F   f surf   → F
   a click   → G   g send   → E
   b enter   → C   h connect   → C
   c attach   → D   i save   → B
   d start up   → A   j delete   → B
   e shut down → A

2 **search**: the internet,
   a document, your computer → F
   scan: a document,
   a photo, your computer   → H
   download: a program, a document,
   a photo, a web page   → E
   send: a document,
   a photo, an email, a link → E
   surf: the internet   → F

3 • out   → C   f down → A
   a on   → G   g to   → F
   b up   → G   h on   → A
   c down → G   i off → A
   d to   → C   j in   → C
   e up   → A

> Now go to page 19. Test yourself again.

Answers to Test it again

1

2 ~~posted~~ sent; ~~enclosing~~ attaching;
   ~~scroll into~~ scroll down; ~~press on~~
   click on; ~~surf to~~ go to; ~~write~~ enter;
   ~~erase~~ delete; ~~put away~~ save;
   ~~attaching~~ connecting; ~~watching~~
   surfing

Fix it notes

A Use *start up* and *shut down* to
   describe how you start and finish
   using a computer. You *switch*
   computers, printers, scanners, etc.
   on and *off*.

B Use *save* and *delete* when you're
   talking about keeping or throwing
   away documents.

C You *connect to* the internet. You *log
   into* and *out of* accounts on the
   internet. You *enter* a password.

D When you send a document or
   photo with an email, you *attach* it.
   Don't use *enclose*.

E You *send* and *receive* emails,
   documents, photos, etc. You
   download files, programs and
   emails from the internet.

F You *surf* and *search* the internet.
   Surfing means looking at, *searching*
   means looking for particular
   information. You *go to* a webpage
   or website.

G You *scroll up* and *down* a page to
   see what's at the top or bottom. You
   click on a link, icon, folder, file, etc.

H You *scan* documents, photos, etc. on
   a scanner. You can also *scan* your
   computer to look for a file or a virus.

> For more information, see the
> Review page opposite.

ℹ Review

Connections You *connect to* the internet. This means that your computer dials the telephone number, then you're *connected to* the internet. You can have a *dial-up* connection, where the computer uses the same line as your telephone, or a *broadband* connection, which is much quicker and increasingly common. *Wi-Fi* is a system that uses radio waves rather than wires to connect to and send information on the internet. Most new computers can now have a *wireless connection* – a connection that works using these radio waves.

Surfing and searching When you're on the internet, you can *surf* or *search*. *Surfing* is looking at pages on the internet, perhaps just for fun. *Searching* is looking for a particular bit of information. To do this, you might use a *search engine* – a website which scans lots of other websites to match the words you type into it as your *search term(s)*. When your search term is found on another site, it's called a *match* (the terms *match* each other).
The search engine came up with 3,000,482 matches; my search term was too vague.

EXTRA TIPS
Note that lots of new words have been invented because of the internet. For example, there's a verb *to google* which means to search for information on the Google website. If you're not sure of their meanings, look them up in a recently-published dictionary or on the internet itself.
I googled 'petroleum resources' and found exactly what I was looking for.

You *download* web pages, programs, documents, etc. from the internet. If you make them available on the internet, you *upload* them. You *go to* or *visit* a website or web page. You use a *link* or *hyperlink* when you are in a web page, email or document, and there's a line or image you can click on to take you to another web page.
Every time I try to download this document, I get an error message.
Visit our site by clicking the link below.

You *scroll up* and *down* a web page or document to see what's at the top or bottom. You *log into* and *out of* accounts that you have on the internet, e.g. email accounts. To do this, you usually need to *enter* a password.
Scroll up and you'll see the company's contact details.
I'm just going to log into my account to see if I've got any new emails.

Email You *send* and *receive* emails. You also *check* your email when you want to see if you have any new messages.
Check your email when you get to work.

You can send *attachments* with emails. These may be photos, documents or sound files. You *attach* these files *to* an email. You can describe a file as being *attached*. Don't use the verb *enclose* – you use this to talk about documents that you send in a letter, by post.
Please find attached the sales report for January.
Charles has sent some photos as attachments so we can assess the site.

Organization You *switch* computers, printers, scanners, etc. *on* and *off*. This means that you connect them to the electricity supply. You *start up* and *shut down* your computer to start and finish using it.

You *open* and *close* programs, files, folders and documents. When you want to keep things like documents, you *save* them. When you want to throw them away, you *delete* them. If you want to keep files or emails that you don't need to look at very often, you can *archive* them.
There's too much stuff on this computer. I need to delete some of it.
My email automatically archives messages that are more than three months old.

Emailing

Test it ✓

1 Choose the correct pairs of words to complete the sentences.

inbox/delete   sent/sent items   attached/saved   bcc/blind copy   ~~open/junk mail~~
address/forward   attachment/re-send   copy/cc   retrieve/trash

Do not ...*open*............... any messages from Flogit Inc. They're
...*junk mail*.......... and contain viruses.

a Please find ...*attached*.... the revised report, ...*saved*...... as a Word
document.

b You've got hundreds of messages in your ...*inbox*....... . You should
....*delete*...... the ones that you don't need.

c I haven't got Joe's email ...*address*.... . Can you ...*forward* this
message to him?

d I couldn't open the ...*attachment*.. Could you ...*re-send*... it in a
different format?

e A What does ......*bcc*...... mean?
    B '...*blind copy*..' You can copy a message to people without their
       names appearing in the message.

f You can check if an email was ...*sent*........ by looking in your
...*sent items*...

g A Oh, no! I've deleted an email by mistake.
    B Don't worry. You can ...*retrieve*... it from the ....*trash*..... if you
       haven't emptied it.

h If you want to ...*copy*..... a message to someone, add their address in
the ...*cc*........... section.

2 Find and correct the mistake in each sentence.

If you give me your email ~~name~~, I'll send you a copy
of the photos. ...*address*...........

a I need to email ~~to~~ my boss to give him the news. ....

b I'm enclosing the report with this email. ...*attaching*...

c I'm copying Miles (in) this message as the information is
relevant to him. ...*in on*...........

d If you hit 'answer all', you can send a message to everyone
who was copied in. *REPLY*

e I'm afraid I haven't received ~~of~~ any of your emails. ....

f I can't stand this trash mail. I get hundreds of stupid
messages a day. *JUNK*

g Please send ~~an email~~ *to* them to explain the changes. ....

h Please reply *to* this message to confirm receipt. ....

GO to page 24 and check your answers.

22

Test it again ✔

1 Match **a–k** to **1–11**.

a I couldn't open the email –   1 to attach the file so here it is.   a *11*
b Don't forget to copy   2 you hit 'reply all'?   b *9*
c Please find attached   3 to the hotel to make the booking.   c *10*
d The circulation list is confidential   4 it isn't in my sent items.   d *6*
e Nobody else got your message. Did   5 to this message asap.   e *2*
f Is it possible to retrieve a message   6 so please bcc everyone.   f *7*
g Have you emailed   7 if you haven't emptied the trash?   g *8*
h Sorry. I forgot   8 Space Designs yet?   h *1*
i Please reply   9 Mr Davies in on the report.   i *5*
j I don't think the message was sent as   10 the figures you requested.   j *4*
k I sent an email   11 the attachment was too big.   k *3*

2 Choose the correct forms of the verbs to complete the email.

~~send~~ ~~forward~~ ~~delete~~ ~~re-send~~ ~~open~~ ~~email~~ ~~attach~~ ~~receive~~ ~~copy~~

To:	M.Hunt@enterpriseskies.com
From:	Andrea.Rawson@correctile.co.uk
Subject:	Update and cost reports

Hi Mike

Thanks for *emailing* me. Hope all's well with you. I ᵃ HAVE just SENT the designers an updated schedule. I ᵇ COPIED you in so I hope you HAVE ᶜ RECEIVED it. If you're happy with the new dates, please ᵈ FORWARD the message to the freelancers on the project, as I don't have their contact details. I ᵉ ATTACH my report on costs to this message. I hope you can ᶠ OPEN the attachment, as I know you had a problem last time. Let me know if I need to ᵍ RE-SEND

Cheers

Andrea

PS Can you let me have directions to the designers' office? I ʰ DELETED their message yesterday by mistake and I've just emptied the trash!

23

Fix it

Answers to Test it

Check your answers. Wrong answer?
Read the right Fix it note to find out why.

1 ● open/junk mail   → B, E
  a attached/saved   → B
  b inbox/delete   → A, E
  c address/forward   → A, C
  d attachment/re-send → B, C
  e bcc/Blind copy   → D
  f sent/sent items   → C, A
  g retrieve/trash   → E, A
  h copy/cc   → D

2 ● ~~name~~   address → A
  a ~~email to my boss~~
    email my boss   → F
  b ~~enclosing~~   attaching → B
  c ~~in this message~~
    in on/into this message → F
  d ~~'answer all'~~   'reply all' → C
  e ~~received of~~   received → F
  f ~~trash mail~~   junk mail → E
  g ~~email them~~   email to
    them/them an email   → F
  h ~~reply this message~~
    reply to this message   → F

Now go to page 23. Test yourself again.

Answers to Test it again

1 **a** 11 **b** 9 **c** 10 **d** 6 **e** 2 **f** 7
  g 8   **h** 1 **i** 5 **j** 4 **k** 3

2 **a** have/'ve ... sent
  b copied/have copied
  c received/have received
  d forward
  e am/'m attaching OR attach
  f open
  g re-send
  h deleted

Fix it notes

A To send a message you need the person's email *address*. Email has a range of mailboxes: the *inbox* for received messages, the *sent* or *sent items* for sent messages and the *trash* for messages that you no longer need.

B You can *send* or *attach* other files with an email. The noun is *attachment*. You *save* an attachment in a format that the other person can read and they then *open* the attachment.

C You *send* an email when you have finished writing it. If it isn't received, you may have to *re-send*. You can *forward* a message *to* someone who was not on the original list. If you choose the *'reply all'* option, you answer everyone on the original list.

D You can *copy* the message to someone by adding addresses in the *cc* section; you can copy a message to people without their names appearing in the message by adding addresses in the *bcc* (*blind copy*) section.

E You *delete* a message that you no longer need. It goes in the *trash* but you can *retrieve* it (get it back) if you haven't emptied the trash. *Junk mail* is advertising and other information you did not ask for and do not want.

F You *email someone* or *send an email to* someone. You *receive* or *get* emails. You *reply to* a message. You *copy* someone *in/on* a message.

For more information, see the Review page opposite. ▷

ⓘ Review

Organizing email *Email* is short for *electronic mail*. To send a message to someone you need their email *address*. You *send* an email when you have finished writing it. If it isn't received, you may have to *re-send*.
Let me have the correct address and I'll re-send the email immediately.

Email has a range of mailboxes: the *inbox* for received messages, the *sent/sent items* for sent messages and the *trash* for messages that you no longer need. You can also *save* an unfinished message in the *drafts* mailbox and go back to it later.
I saved my message as a draft because I needed to add some figures the next day. Check your sent items to see if the email has gone.

Attachments You can *send* or *attach* other files to an email. The noun is *attachment*. You *save an attachment* in a format that the other person can read and they then *open the attachment*. You can use these expressions to say that you have added an attachment:
Please find attached .. (formal) or *I'm attaching ...*
I'm attaching the minutes of last week's meeting. Let me know if I've missed anything.

⚠ Don't confuse these expressions with *Please find enclosed ..* or *I'm enclosing ...*, which are used when sending other documents with a letter through the post.

Forwarding and copying You can *forward* a message to someone who was not on the original list. You also use these verbs to ask people to do something with your email: *Please send/forward/copy this email to ...* If you choose the *reply all* option, you answer everyone on the original list.
When you've checked the announcement, could you please forward it to your department?
Katie Johnson hit 'reply all' by mistake, so the whole company got her itinerary.

You can *copy* the message to someone by adding their address in the *cc* section; you can copy a message to people without their names appearing in the message by adding addresses in the *bcc* (*blind copy*) section.
Nick sent me a blind copy of his email about the budget cuts.

Deleting messages You *delete* a message that you no longer need. It goes in the *trash* but you can *retrieve* it (get it back) if you haven't emptied the trash. *Junk mail* or *spam* is advertising and other information you did not ask for and do not want. Modern computers often have a filter to limit the amount of junk mail that gets through.
I used to get about ten junk mails a day but now I rarely get any.

Prepositions You *email someone or send an email to someone.* You *receive* or *get* emails. You *reply to* a message. You *copy* someone *in* on or *into* a message.
Email me when you get to your hotel.
I copied you in on an email I sent to Sam.

Starting and ending emails You start emails in various different ways, depending on how formal you need to be. In formal emails, for example to people you've never met or haven't contacted before, it's common to start with *Dear* + the person's name. When you're writing emails to people you know, e.g. colleagues, business contacts, you can use *Hi* + person's name, or just *Hi*. Some people just use the person's name:

> *Dear Mr Rogers*
> *I'm writing with reference to ...*

> *Hi Joe*
> *Thanks for your phone call ...*

> *Mark*
> *The meeting next week ...*

Common endings for emails include: *Kind regards, Regards, Best wishes, I look forward (to meeting you), All the best, Best.*

Formal letters

Test it ✓

1 Look at the extracts. Circle the correct option, **A** or **B**.

A Dear Mr/Ms   **(B)** Dear Sir/Madam

a (A) *Dear Sir*   **B** *Dear Sir*
   Yours faithfully   *Yours sincerely*

b (A) I am enclosing a copy of my CV.   **B** There's a copy of my CV inside.

c (A)~~×~~ the fifth of November 2006   **(B)** 5 November 2006

d A
12 Park Road
Oxford OX12 6DQ

The Manager
Solutions Ltd
192 Northern Avenue
Bolton
MU3 5QT

B
The Manager
Solutions Ltd
192 Northern Avenue
Bolton
MU3 5QT

12 Park Road
Oxford OX12 6DQ

e (A) Yours sincerely,
David Jackson
David Jackson

B Yours sincerely,
David Jackson

f A Ms Walters
Many thanks for your letter of

(B) Dear Ms Walters
Thank you for your letter of

2 Circle the correct option.

Write the date (before)/after the address of the person you're writing to.
a You (can)/can't use 'Dear Mr or Mrs' to start a letter.
b (Enc.)/cc. at the bottom of a letter means there are other documents sent with it.
c Use 'Yours (sincerely)/faithfully' if you start 'Dear Ms Clarke'.
d You (need)/don't need to include your address in a business letter.
e You (can)/can't use a person's job title in a business letter.
f You (need)/don't need to divide business letters into paragraphs.

GO to page 28 and check your answers.

Test it again ✔

1 Read the letter. Decide whether the statements are true or false.

> *30*
> ~~the thirtieth of~~ September
>
> Philip Josephs
> Star Studios Ltd
> 342 Newman's Road
> London
> W2 3JR
>
> Rose Cottage
> Lower Swell
> Worcestershire
> WR1 2EJ
>
> Dear Mr Philip Josephs
>
> You may remember that I wrote to you in August asking if you
> would kindly pay the invoice I sent you last December. I'm
> afraid that I still have not receieved payment for the recording
> work I did. You'll find a copy of my invoice inside this letter.
> I am extremely disappointed that your company has not replied to
> my letters or dealt with my invoice. It is, after all, nine
> months since I carried out the work for you. I would be greatful
> if you would attend to this matter urgently.
>
> Yours ~~faithfully~~ sincerely
> *Jodie Tootle*

		TRUE	FALSE
	The punctuation in the addresses is correct.	✓	☐
a	There are no spelling mistakes.	☒	☒
b	There is something missing in the date.	☒	☐
c	The paragraphing is excellent.	☐	☒
d	The start of the letter is incorrect.	☒	☐
e	The end of the letter should say 'Yours faithfully'.	☐	☒
f	The order of addresses is correct.	☐	☒
g	There is something missing at the bottom of the page.	☒	☒
h	The date is correctly written.	☐	☒
i	The date is in the right place.	☐	☒
j	'Inside this letter' is an incorrect way of saying 'enclosed'.	☒	☐

2 Look again at the letter. Find and correct the mistakes.

Fix it

Answers to Test it

Check your answers. Wrong answer?
Read the right Fix it note to find out why.

1 • B → A			**d** A → C	
a A → A			**e** A → E	
b A → B			**f** B → F	
c B → D				

2 • before	→ D
a can't	→ F
b Enc.	→ B
c sincerely	→ A
d need	→ C
e can	→ C
f need	→ G

Now go to page 27. Test yourself again.

Answers to Test it again

1 a False	**f** False
b True	**g** True
c False	**h** False
d True	**i** False
e False	**j** True

2 a the year is missing from the date
(30 September 2007 OR 30/09/07)

b the writer's address should come
first, then the date, then the
recipient's address

c Mr Philip Josephs
Dear Mr Josephs

d receeieved   received

e You'll find a copy of my invoice
inside this letter.
I enclose/Please find enclosed a
copy of my invoice.

f a new paragraph is needed after
'... inside this letter.'

g a new paragraph is needed after
'... work for you.'

h greatful   grateful

i faithfully   sincerely

j a typed name is needed under the
signature

Fix it notes

A If you start a letter *Dear Sir* or *Dear Madam*, you end with *Yours faithfully*. If you start a letter *Dear + person's name*, you end with *Yours sincerely*. Use *Dear Sir/Madam* when you don't know the name of the person you're writing to.

B Use *enclose* when you send other documents in the same envelope as your letter. You sometimes see the abbreviations *enc.* or *encs.* at the bottom of a letter. Use *cc.* when you send a copy of the letter to someone else.

C Put your address before, not after, the address of the person you're writing to. If you don't know the person's name, use their job title or a general job title, e.g. *The Manager*.

D Write dates like this: *5 July 2006* (not *the fifth of July*). It's increasingly acceptable to use numbers, e.g. *05/07/06*. Write the date before the address of the other person.

E Sign your letter by hand but type your name below your signature.

F Always start a formal letter with *Dear*. Don't just write the person's name. Use *Mr, Mrs* or *Ms* before the surname, e.g. *Dear Ms Walters*.

G Start a new point with a new paragraph. Always check your spelling and grammar before sending the letter.

For more information, see the
Review page opposite.

ⓘ Review

Starting and ending If you start a letter *Dear Sir* or *Dear Madam*, you end with *Yours faithfully*. If you start a letter *Dear +* person's name, you end with *Yours sincerely*. Note that some people don't use *Yours* at all, they just write *Sincerely*. In American English, it's often *Sincerely yours* or just *Sincerely*. You need to use *Dear Sir/Madam* when you don't know the name of the person you're writing to. Always start a formal letter with *Dear*. Don't just write the person's name. You use *Mr, Mrs,* or *Ms* before the surname, e.g. *Dear Mr King*. Remember that it's often better to use *Ms* for women, especially if you don't know whether a woman is married or not. (See p77, 'Cultural matters'.)

Addresses Put your address before, not after, the address of the person you're writing to. If you're using your company's letterhead (printed company paper which includes the company name, address, etc.), the address will already be on it, so you don't need to type it again. If you don't know the person's name, either use their job title if you know it, or a general job title, e.g. *The Manager, The Chief Executive*.

Dates Remember to date your letter. You write the date before the address of the person you're writing to, but after your own address. You write dates like this: *5 July 2006* (not the fifth of July). It's increasingly acceptable to use numbers, e.g. *05/07/06*.

Note that in American English, dates are written differently. You put the month before the day: *July 5, 2006* or *07/05/2006*. It's safer not to use numbers in case there's confusion over the months and days.

Other documents You use *enclose* when you send other documents (e.g. your CV, a copy of an earlier letter, an invoice) in the same envelope as your letter. The noun is *enclosure*. You use *Please find enclosed* (formal) or *I enclose* or *I'm enclosing* (less formal). You sometimes see the abbreviation *enc.* or *encs.* at the bottom of a letter. This tells you that there are other documents with the letter.

Other recipients You write *cc.* (carbon copy) and a person's name when you send a copy of the letter to another person, e.g. *cc. David Carpenter*.

Signing Always sign your letter by hand but remember to type your full name underneath your signature.

EXTRA TIPS

If you can't sign a letter for some reason, someone else can sign on your behalf. In this case they sign their name but put *pp.* in front of your typed name.

Yours sincerely,

Adrian Leech

pp. *Michael Harmsworth*

Paragraphing Start a new point with a new paragraph – don't run everything together. Always check your spelling and grammar before sending the letter.

Note that you often use the following phrases in formal letters:

With reference to [your letter of 15 March/the invoice you sent on 9 July)

Please find enclosed NOT ~~attached~~

I'm writing about/with reference to/in response to

I would be (very) grateful

I look forward to (hearing from you at your earliest convenience/soon)

Job applications

Test it ✔

1 Circle the correct option.

I asked if the company had any (vacancies)/offers in the IT department.

a I look at the job advices/(ads) in the newspaper every week.

b Why don't you look/search the job websites on the net?

c Have you sent your qualifications/(CV) to that company yet?

d I was (headhunted)/fired for my job so I didn't have to send in an application.

e I've sent about 100 (application)/applying letters but I still haven't got a reply.

f I wrote to the company but they aren't (recruiting)/employing at the moment.

g My interview was short as I was the last interviewer/(interviewee) that day.

h It's incredible – there were 112 competitors/(candidates) for the sales job.

2 Choose a word from each box to complete the sentences.

selection	interview	~~employment~~	~~human~~	character	~~psychometric~~	~~handwriting~~

panel	~~tests~~	~~agency~~	analysis	resources	~~process~~	reference

I tried to form my letters clearly for the _handwriting analysis_ but I don't know what the test will say about me.

a There were two women and one man on the _interview panel_

b The _selection process_ was really long – it took the company three months to find the right person. _employment_

c Why don't you register at the _agency_ – they can send you information about new jobs.

d I'm looking for a job. Would you mind writing a _reference_ for me? _character_

e After the interview, the person from _HR_ explained the pension system at the company.

f Some firms use _psych... tests_ to find out about people's personality.

3 Circle the correct option, A or B.

I've registered ...... Temp Nation Recruitment. **A** for (**B**) with

a I replied ...... an advertisement for a job in Japan. (**A**) to **B** of

b Please fill ...... this application form. **A** up (**B**) in

c It's easy to feel depressed if you're ...... work. **A** out (**B**) out of

d They offered me the job but I turned it .... **A** off **B** down

e I'm sorry but we aren't taking ...... any new staff. (**A**) on **B** up

f How many jobs have you applied ......? **A** to (**B**) for

GO to page 32 and check your answers.

Test it again ✔

1 **Correct the mistakes in bold in the dialogue.**

MAX   Hi Paula. How's the job hunting going?

PAULA Oh, OK. I applied **to** a job in sales and I had an **ᵃvacancy** last week. There were about ten other **ᵇinterviewers** sitting outside the interview room when I got there, so there's a lot of competition.

MAX   I'm sure you'll do well. I was impressed with your **ᶜqualifications** when I read it. Do you need a character **ᵈreport**? I can write one for you if you like.

PAULA Oh, thanks, Max. I'll let you know if they ask for one. The next stage of the selection **ᵉpanel** is **ᶠpsychiatric** tests.

MAX   Oh, I've never done those before, but I had a **ᵍhandwritten** analysis once. They said I was a dreamer and couldn't take risks – a bit strange as I now have my own company!

PAULA Yes, that is odd. Anyway, I must go now. I want to **ʰsearch at** the on-line job ads.

MAX   OK, see you soon and good luck.

a *for* / *Interview*   c *CV*   f *psychometric*
b *candidates*   d *reference*   g *handwriting*
                     e *process*   h *look at*

2 **Choose the correct forms of the verbs to complete the sentences.**

~~recruit~~   ~~reply to~~   ~~look at~~   ~~fill in~~   ~~turn down~~   ~~register with~~   headhunt

If you ....*looked at*..... the ads in the paper, you'd find lots of job opportunities.

a It's a good idea to *register with* an employment agency.

b I've never been *headhunted* for a job. I've always had to apply.

c Please *fill in* this form in black ink.

d I *replied to* an ad for a job in accounts but I didn't get an interview.

e I was going to take the job but I *turned* it *down* because I had a better offer.

f Unfortunately, we don't have any vacancies so we *are* not *recruiting* at the moment.

Answers to Test it

Check your answers. Wrong answer?
Read the right Fix it note to find out why.

1 • vacancies → C
  a ads → A
  b search → A
  c CV → B
  d headhunted → C
  e application → B
  f recruiting → C
  g interviewee → D
  h candidates → D

2 • handwriting analysis → E
  a interview panel → D
  b selection process → D
  c employment agency → A
  d character reference → B
  e Human Resources → F
  f psychometric tests → E

3 • B → A   d B → C
  a A → B   e A → C
  b B → B   f B → B
  c B → A

◀ Now go to page 31. Test yourself again.

Answers to Test it again

1 a vacancy   interview
  b interviewers
     interviewees/candidates
  c qualifications   CV
  d report   reference
  e panel   process
  f psychiatric   psychometric
  g handwritten   handwriting
  h search at   search/look at

2 a register with
  b headhunted
  c fill in
  d replied to
  e turned ... down
  f 're ... recruiting

🔧 Fix it notes

A If you don't have a job, you're *out of work*. You find information about a job in an *ad* (*advert/advertisement*). You can also *search* or *look at* websites and *register with* an *employment agency*.

B You *reply to* a job advert. You *apply for* a job by writing an *application* letter and/or *filling in* a form. A *CV* lists your qualifications and experience. A statement from someone who knows you to support your application is a *character reference*.

C A job that is available is a *vacancy*. If a company wants new staff, they *recruit* or *take on* people. If you are *headhunted*, a person/company asks you to leave your job to work for another organization. If you decide not to accept a job, you *turn* it *down*.

D The people who interview you are the *interview panel*. The people who interview are *interviewers* and the people who are interviewed are *interviewees*. People who are competing for a job are *candidates*. The stages of finding a person for a job make up the *selection process*.

E Companies use *psychometric tests* or *handwriting analysis* to test candidates' ability to think and to analyse their personality.

F The *Human Resources* department helps to choose new employees and explains the systems in a company.

For more information, see the Review page opposite. ▷

ⓘ Review

Finding a job If you don't have a job, you are *out of work* or *unemployed*. You can find information about a job in an *ad* (or *advert*(*advertisement*), often in a newspaper. The section of the newspaper with jobs is sometimes called *Situations vacant*. Advertisements also appear on company noticeboards or in special monthly job bulletins. You can also *register with* an *employment agency* to find out about new jobs. If you use the internet, you *search* or *look at* websites.
Mark's been unemployed for nearly a year. He keeps looking at the job ads in The Times but there's nothing suitable. He should register with an employment agency or look at Monster.com.

Applying for a job You *reply to* a job advert. You *apply for* a job by writing an *application* letter and/or *filling in* an application form. As part of your application you may need to provide a *CV* (curriculum vitae) with your *qualifications* and work experience. The CV is the document itself; *qualifications* are things like degrees or diplomas received after a period of study/training. You may also need to provide professional *references* from a previous employer and/or a *character reference* – a statement from someone who knows you to support your application. The people who write references are called *referees*. If you are *headhunted*, a person/company asks you to leave your job to work for another organization. The person or company is called a *headhunter*.

▬▬ Note that in American English you *fill out* (not *fill in*) an *application form*, *questionnaire*, etc. and you use the word *resume* rather than *CV*.
A job that is available is a *vacancy*. If a company wants new staff, they *recruit* or *take on* people. Note the word order with *take on*:
They decided not to take on any new designers. OR *They decided not to take any new designers on.*
They decided not to take them on.
NOT *They decided not to take on them.* (The object is a pronoun.)

If you decide not to accept a job, you *turn it down*. Note the word order with *turn down*:
He turned the job down.
OR *He turned down the job.*
He turned it down.
NOT *He turned down it.* (The object is a pronoun.)

Interviews and selection The people who interview you are the *interviewers*. Often there may be several people interviewing you at the same time. They are the *interview panel*. The people who are interviewed are *interviewees*. You can *attend* or *go to* an *interview*. People who are competing for a job are *candidates*. The stages of finding a person for a job make up the *selection process*.
The selection process for the job was tough. There were over thirty candidates competing for two positions. We all had to attend an interview with an interview panel.

The *Human Resources* department (often called just *HR*) helps to choose candidates. It often also deals with training and staff problems. In some companies, this department interviews new employees and explains the systems in a company to any new workers. HR is called *Personnel* in some companies. Personnel is another word for staff.

Tests Companies use *psychometric tests* or *handwriting analyses* to test candidates' ability to think and analyse their personality. These are becoming quite common in some companies, as employers believe these tests reveal candidates' strengths and weaknesses.
Every time I go to an interview these days I have to do a psychometric test.

Promotion and unemployment

Test it ✔

1 Is the meaning of each word or phrase in the set the same or different?

		SAME	DIFFERENT

He was { dismissed / fired / sacked } for stealing from the company.   ✔ ☐

a I've been { out of work / unemployed / retired } for over a year now.   ☐ ☒

b Franco { was promoted / was demoted / got promotion } to section leader.   ☐ ☒

c I hope I'm not { dismissed / made redundant / given early retirement } from the factory.   ☒ ☒

d I hope my manager doesn't { hand in her notice. / resign. / quit. }   ☒ ☐

e The directors are going to { restructure / downsize / close } the company.   ☐ ☒

2 Circle the correct option.

There may be (redundancies)/redundants if we can't cut costs.

a I'm not sure why I wasn't promotion/(promoted.)
b We have an (appraisal)/appraised scheme in this company.
c I wonder if we'll get a salary rise/(increase.)
d If the company downsizes, I'll take early retired/(retirement.)
e (lost)/missed my job because the company had financial problems.
f We're pleased with your progress and we think you're ready to move to a more junior/(senior) position.
g Why did you resign (from)/for your last job?
h What did your boss say when you were (appraised)/appraisal?
i This letter asks all employees over 60 to agree/(accept) early retirement.
j Do you get a wages/(pay) rise with your promotion?
k I want more responsibility so I'm going for promoted/(promotion.)
l They're giving us a pretty good redundancy packet/(package.)

GO to page 36 and check your answers.

Test it again ✔

1 **Number the lines of the text in the correct order.**

I thought it was time that I got ... 1..
a promoted. So anyway, I don't want to hand in 11
b appraised under a new performance review. Six months 6..
c promotion. She said I wasn't ready for a more senior 7..
d promotion and a salary increase. So I had a 2...
e later, I had my appraisal but my boss didn't agree to my 7.
f meeting with my boss and said that I wanted to go 3.
g my appraisal. In my company all the employees are 5.
h for promotion. She told me that I had to wait until 4..
i position so she wouldn't allow me to have a pay 8..
j my notice, but I'm not sure what to do now. 12.
k rise. I was upset because I wanted to be ....

2 **Change the words in brackets to form words connected with promotion and unemployment.**

We have to become more efficient so we're going to ...*restructure*..... (structure).

a I'm afraid that my best designer has decided to .... (sign).
b We need to arrange a time for your .... (appraise).
c They've offered me early .... (retire) but I don't really want to take it.
d The longer you're .... (employ), the more difficult it becomes to find a job.
e How many .... (redundant) were there in your department?
f Why were you .... (miss) from your last job?
g If we .... (down), how many people will lose their jobs?
h What are my chances of .... (promote), do you think?

Fix it

Now go to page 35. Test yourself again.

Answers to Test it

Check your answers. Wrong answer?
Read the right Fix it note to find out why.

1 • same → B
a different → A, C
b different → E
c different → B, C
d same → B
e different → D

2 • redundancies → B
a promoted → E
b appraisal → F
c increase → E
d retirement → C
e lost → A
f senior → E
g from → B
h appraised → F
i accept → C
j pay → E
k promotion → E
l package → B

Answers to Test it again

1 a 11   e 7   i 9
b 6   f 3   j 12
c 8   g 5   k 10
d 2   h 4

2 a resign
b appraisal
c retirement
d unemployed
e redundancies
f dismissed
g downsize
h promotion

Fix it notes

A If you don't have a job, you're *out of work/unemployed*. You *lose* (not *miss*) *your job* if you have to stop working at a particular place.

B Use *be dismissed/fired/sacked* if you do something wrong and lose your job. Use *be made redundant* if there is no longer a job for you. The noun is *redundancy* and a *redundancy package* is the money and benefits you receive. Use *resign/quit/hand in your notice* when you leave your current job. You resign *from* a job.

C If you finish your working life, you *retire*. The noun is *retirement* and the adjective is *retired*. Companies sometimes *give early retirement* to staff who haven't yet reached retirement age; people can *accept/ take early retirement*.

D Use *restructure* if a company reorganizes itself. Use *downsize* if it reduces the number of workers. Use *close* if it stops altogether.

E Use *be promoted/get promotion* if you move to a more *senior* position; use *be demoted* if you move to a more *junior* position. You can *go for/apply for promotion*. If you get more money, it's a *pay rise/salary increase*.

F Some companies have an *appraisal scheme/system* in which employees' performance is reviewed. You can *have an appraisal* or *be appraised*.

For more information, see the Review page opposite.

ℹ Review

Unemployment If you don't have a job, you are *out of work/unemployed*. You *lose* (not *miss*) *your job* if you have to stop working at a particular place. In many countries, you might go *on the dole*. This means you receive money from the state while you're looking for another job.
I've never been out of work.
I lost my job at the PR company.
For the first time, I'm on the dole.

Losing jobs You use *be dismissed/fired/sacked* or *get the sack* if you do something wrong and you lose your job. *Be dismissed/fired* is more formal than *be sacked/get the sack.*
Tim was sacked for poor performance.

You use *be made redundant* if there is no longer a job for you. The noun is *redundancy* and a *redundancy package* is the money and benefits you receive. A company negotiates a *redundancy settlement* with its workers. (The *settlement* covers all the workers to be made redundant, as a whole; the *package* refers to each worker individually.) If it needs to downsize, a company may ask some of its workers to take *voluntary redundancy*: those who will easily find another job or who are close to retirement choose to leave. You use *be laid off* if you are told not to come to work temporarily because there is not enough to do.
Production was moved to China and I was made redundant.
The packers were laid off for a month.

Leaving a job You use *resign/hand in your notice/quit* when you want to leave your current job, and when you officially inform your company that you want to change jobs. You resign *from* a job. You use *leave* when you actually finish.
I'm going to hand in my notice today.
We're sorry that you're leaving.

▬▬▬ Note that *quit* is especially common in American English, where it can be used formally. *Quit* is informal in British English.

Retirement If you finish your working life, you *retire*. The noun is *retirement* and the adjective is *retired*. Companies sometimes *give/offer early retirement* to staff who haven't yet reached retirement age; people can *accept/take* early retirement.
Most people retire at the age of 65.
Have a happy retirement.
What will you do when you're retired?
If they offer you early retirement, will you take it?

Restructuring You use *restructure* if a company reorganizes its management/way of working to make it more efficient. You use *downsize* if a company reduces the number of workers. You use *close* if a company stops altogether.
When we restructured, our performance improved significantly.
We need to downsize to be competitive.
ECT closed after 100 years of trading.

Appraisal and promotion Some companies have an *appraisal scheme/system* in which employees' performance is reviewed. You can *have an appraisal* or *be appraised*.
We're introducing an appraisal scheme.
When are you having your appraisal/being appraised?

You use *be promoted/get promotion* if you move to a higher (= more *senior*) position in a company. You use *be demoted* if you are moved to a lower (= more *junior*) position. You can *go for/apply for promotion*. If you get promoted quickly, you *get on well* in a company. If you get more money, you get a *pay rise/salary increase*.
She's just been promoted.
They offered her a more senior position.
Ed applied for promotion and got it.
I don't feel I'm getting on well here.
All staff will get a pay rise in May.

Working conditions

Test it ✔

1 Choose a word from each box to complete the sentences.

> work ~~annual~~ quiet parking air meeting gym leisure open
>
> membership plan facilities ~~leave~~ stations spaces room conditioning room

We get five weeks' ...*annual leave*....... .

a I need to concentrate but it's so noisy in this part of the office. We need a
....

b There aren't any .... where I work – nowhere to spend time with colleagues after work.

c I never drive to work as there aren't enough ....

d I don't mind working in an .... office but it can be noisy.

e The .... has broken down again. It's hard to work in this heat.

f My .... is paid for by the company so I play squash about three times a week.

g The sales team are waiting for us in the ....

h It's going to get very crowded on this floor – they're adding another ten
....

2 Circle the correct option.

Annie has broken her leg, so she's on ill/sick leave until the new year.

a We don't have a canteen on/off site but it's a short walk to the nearest café.

b My company publishes travel books and we get 40% staff sales/discount on any book we order.

c I have to pay a lot for childcare as we don't have a crèche/babysitter at work.

d It's great – we've got our own in-office/in-house masseur now so we can get a neck massage at our desks.

e Our company subsidizes/subsidiaries the cost of train travel to work.

f We entertain clients a lot but we get the money back in/on expenses.

g I transport/commute to work every day but my boss doesn't pay any of my travel costs.

h I worked last weekend, so I'm taking time out/off in lieu.

GO to page 40 and check your answers.

Test it again ✔

1 What facilities would help these people at work?

All the cafés and restaurants near the office are
so expensive.   .subsidized canteen....

a   I don't know who's going to look after my children
    during the school holidays.   ....

b   It's a shame there's nowhere for us to get together
    after work.   ....

c   I'd love to order our latest camera but it's very
    expensive.   ....

d   I'm seeing clients in ten minutes but we've got to
    have our discussion in the reception area.   ....

e   It costs me a fortune every week to leave my car
    near the office.   ....

f   I've been here a week and I've had to sit at three
    different desks.   ....

g   The phones haven't stopped ringing on this floor
    all morning and I need to finish my report.   ....

h   I'd like to get more exercise but the sports club
    near work is so overpriced.   ....

2 Find and correct ten mistakes in the speech.

> *open plan*
> So, let me tell you a bit about the company. All the floors are ~~open-space~~,
> so there are lots of opportunities for communication. All areas of the
> office have air-conditioned. We offer subscribed travel for all our
> managers, so you can commuter to work much more cheaply. Travel
> abroad and client entertainment can be claimed on expensive. There is
> also a staff discredit on all the products we manufacture. We have a gym
> and a doctor on-house and there are several in-site experts to help with
> stress management. And, finally, all employees get four weeks' year leave
> and you get paid sickness leave. You can also take time off in place if you
> work evenings or weekends.

Fix it

Answers to Test it

Check your answers. Wrong answer?
Read the right Fix it note to find out why.

1
- annual leave → G
- **a** quiet room → C
- **b** leisure facilities → B
- **c** parking spaces → D
- **d** open-plan → A
- **e** air conditioning → C
- **f** gym membership → B
- **g** meeting room → C
- **h** workstations → A

2
- sick → G
- **a** on → F
- **b** discount → E
- **c** crèche → B
- **d** in-house → F
- **e** subsidizes → E
- **f** on → E
- **g** commute → D
- **h** off → G

Now go to page 39. Test yourself again.

Answers to Test it again

1
- **a** crèche
- **b** leisure facilities
- **c** staff discount
- **d** meeting room
- **e** parking space
- **f** workstation
- **g** quiet room
- **h** gym membership

2
- **a** ~~air-conditioned~~ air conditioning
- **b** ~~subscribed~~ subsidized
- **c** ~~commuter~~ commute
- **d** ~~on expensive~~ on expenses
- **e** ~~discredit~~ discount
- **f** ~~on house~~ in-house
- **g** ~~in-site~~ on site
- **h** ~~year~~ annual
- **i** ~~sickness~~ sick
- **j** ~~place~~ lieu

Fix it notes

A Use *open plan* for an office with lots of open space; use *workstation* to refer to someone's desk.

B Use *leisure facilities* to refer to parts of an office where employees can do non-work-related activities; *gym membership* is often a staff benefit paid for by the employer. Some offices have a *crèche* where parents can leave their children.

C Many offices have *air conditioning* to keep the temperature cool. Most floors have *meeting rooms* and some have *quiet rooms*.

D Use *commute to work* to mean 'travel regularly to and from work'. Staff and visitors use *parking spaces*.

E A company *subsidizes* you if it pays part of the cost of travel, meals, etc. The adjective is *subsidized*. You get things *on expenses* if your company pays you back for them. You get a *staff discount* if you buy things produced/provided by your company at a reduced price.

F *On site* refers to things that are part of the office buildings; *in-house* refers to people or things that are in the companys offices.

G *Annual leave* is the holiday you get each year. *Sick leave* is time that you can be away from work due to illness. *Time off in lieu* is holiday you can take because you've worked more than your normal hours.

For more information, see the Review page opposite.

i Review

Offices You use *open plan* to talk about an office with few individual rooms and a lot of open space; you use *workstation* to refer to the desk that a person works at, usually with a computer. Some offices are divided up into *cubicles* or *cubes*. These are individual offices but they don't have doors or ceilings, just four walls.
There are thirty workstations on each open-plan floor.
Carla works in the cube next to mine.

Most modern offices have *air conditioning* to keep the temperature cool enough for people to work. The adjective is *air-conditioned*.
We're moving to air-conditioned offices.

Most workplaces have *meeting rooms* and some have *quiet rooms* if employees might need a special area where they can concentrate.
Next month's tactical planning meeting is in Meeting Room A on the ninth floor.

You use *on site* to refer to things that are part of the office buildings. You use *in-house* to refer to people or things that are in the offices of a company.
Is there a canteen on site?
We have an in-house translator.

Benefits You use *leisure facilities* to refer to parts of an office where employees can relax or do non-work-related activities.
Gym membership is often a staff benefit paid for by the employer.
Does your office have any leisure facilities?
We offer gym membership as part of our package.

Some offices have a *crèche* or *nursery* where parents can leave their children while they are working, though most parents in the UK use private childcare.
Unlike some countries in Europe, few UK offices have a crèche.

Travel and money You use *commute to work* to mean 'travel regularly to and from work'. The person is a *commuter*. Staff and visitors use *parking spaces* in the office car park.

Millions of commuters take the train to work every day.
It takes Pietro about 40 minutes to commute from Brooklyn to Manhattan.

A company *subsidizes* you if it pays part of the cost of travel to work, meals, etc. The adjective is *subsidized*, e.g. *subsidized travel/canteen*, and the noun is *subsidy*.
Is there any subsidy on the staff canteen?
Some of our travel is subsidized because the company has shares in TrainTrack.

You get travel, food, entertainment, etc. *on expenses* if your company pays you back for what you have spent. You get a *staff discount* if you can buy things produced/provided by your company at a reduced price.
I'll pay for lunch as I can claim it on expenses.
You get a staff discount on our books.

Time away from work You use *leave* to talk about time that you are allowed to be away from work. You can use a range of words before *leave*, e.g. *annual, sick, maternity leave*. *Annual leave* is the holiday you get each year. You *book* and then *take* annual leave. *Sick leave* is time that you can be away from work because of illness. *Maternity leave* is the time that a woman is away from work after having a baby. Some companies also offer *paternity leave* to men who become fathers.

You also use *time off* to talk about time when you're allowed not to be at work. You can sometimes take *time off in lieu* if you've worked more than your normal hours.
I'm taking three days off next week.
Don't forget to take your time off in lieu for working late last week.

Note that in American English, time off in lieu is often called *comp days*. *Comp* is short for compensation.
He got a comp day for working at the conference on Saturday.

Pay and benefits

Test it ✔

1 Choose a word from each box to complete the sentences.

> job   income   pay   employer   ~~commission~~   pension
> performance-related   health   salary   pay   company

> slip   car   insurance   career   ~~bonus~~   rise   pay
> scheme   employees   tax   income

Salaries at VGT are low but you get ...*commission*... with each sale and a big annual ..*bonus*........ .

a   Don says his ...JOB..... is OK but he's not sure he can make a .... out of working in telesales.

b   I drive to see clients as part of my job, so I get a ....CAR..... .

c   I can't decide whether to join the company's .... After all, I'm not going to retire for another 30 years!

d   22% of my salary is taken as ....TAX...... before I get paid.

e   The .... told the .... that there would be a change of management.

f   Now that I've got two kids, I really need a .... I'm not earning enough!

g   Your .... shows you how much tax you pay each month.

h   My .... is about €75,000 but my annual .... is slightly more because I have some money invested.

i   I was ill last year, so I was glad that my company gives us ....

j   We have a system of .... – we get extra money if we meet our targets.

2 Circle the correct option.

I only realized how high taxes were when I got my first pay form/**slip**

a   How much can you **earn**/win in IT?

b   What's the weekly **salary**/wage for the bar job?

c   Do you pay revenue/**income** tax?

d   The management can't afford to give us a pay **cut**/rise.

e   I get some nice **perks**/bonuses in my job – a company car and free meals.

f   Everyone has to pay commission/**tax** to the government from their salary.

g   It costs a huge amount to pay our **workforce**/workload.

h   Cash flow is a big problem for people who are **self-employed**/self-employment.

i   We can't accept any more people on to our pension system/**scheme**.

j   Did she get any performance-related salary/**pay** this month?

GO to page 44 and check your answers.

Test it again ✔

① **Choose the correct words to complete the advert.**

salary   workforce   scheme   ~~earn~~   performance-related
career   perks   insurance   company

....._Earn_..... **thousands with**

》》》》》》》FastTrack!》》》》》》

Do you want a **a**................. in sales?

Join our talented **b**................. at *FastTrack Education,* the UK's leading publisher of online learning materials.

We offer a competitive **c**................. with a range of **d**.................
including **e**................. car and health **f**................. . We also
operate a company pension **g**................. and offer **h**.................
pay for hitting our sales targets.

FastTrack Education, PO Box 995, London E1 9YZ
recruitment@fasttrack.edu.uk   www.fasttrack.edu.uk
Recruitment hotline 0888 9876543   **》》》FastTrack!》》**
EDUCATION

② **Find and correct the mistakes in the sentences.**

Even though it's subsidized, health ~~assurance~~ is very expensive.   _insurance_

a   My annual wage is paid directly into my bank account.   ....
b   No one who works can avoid paying tax.   ....
c   One of the perks of the job is that you get discounts on flights.   ....
d   It's a small internet company with about ten or eleven workforce.   ....
e   The workforce went on strike because of the pay cuttings.   ....
f   Sue Dixon doesn't have a regular income because she's
auto-employed.   ....
g   Do you win more in your new job?   ....
h   Do you use an accountant or do you sort out your own tax?   ....
i   The pension scheme is excellent. I suggest you join it.   ....
j   We received a bonus at the end of the year as a thank you
from the management.   ....

Answers to Test it

Check your answers. Wrong answer?
Read the right Fix it note to find out why.

1
- commission, bonus → E
- a job, career → A
- b company car → D
- c pension scheme → D
- d income tax → C
- e employer, employees → A
- f pay rise → D
- g pay slip → C
- h salary, income → B
- i health insurance → D
- j performance-related pay → E

2
- slip → C
- a earn → B
- b wage → B
- c income → C
- d rise → D
- e perks → D
- f tax → C
- g workforce → A
- h self-employed → C
- i scheme → D
- j pay → E

Now go to page 43. Test yourself again.

Answers to Test it again

1
- a career
- b workforce
- c salary
- d perks
- e company
- f insurance
- g scheme
- h performance-related

2
- a ~~wage~~ salary
- b correct
- c correct
- d ~~workforce~~ employees
- e ~~cuttings~~ cut(s)
- f ~~auto-employed~~ self-employed
- g ~~win~~ earn
- h correct
- i correct
- j correct

🔧 Fix it notes

A A *job* is work that you do for money; a *career* is an occupation that you have for a longer time. *Employers* employ people. *Employees* work for an employer. The *workforce* is all the people working in a company.

B You *earn* (not *win*) money for the work that you do. A *wage* is a fixed amount of money, usually paid weekly. A *salary* is a fixed amount of money, agreed annually, and usually paid monthly. Your *income* is the total amount of money you make in a year.

C When you get paid, a *pay slip* shows how your pay is broken down. Usually, the employer takes the *income tax* out of your salary. If you're not employed but you work, you're *self-employed*.

D If your salary is increased/reduced, you get a *pay rise/cut*. *Perks* are benefits such as a *company car*, *health insurance*. A *pension scheme* is a financial plan you and your employer pay into for your retirement.

E *Performance-related pay* is an extra payment for meeting targets; *commission* is payment as a percentage of everything someone sells; a *bonus* is an extra payment on top of your salary/wage.

For more information, see the Review page opposite. ▷

ℹ Review

Jobs and careers You use *job* to talk about work that you do for money but a *career* is a job or occupation that you have for a long time, possibly all your working life. You *have a career in* banking, for example, or you *have a career as* a banker. *I had about six jobs when I was in my twenties, before starting my career in management consultancy.*

Employers and employees *Employers* are people who employ you, so your company or organization is your employer. You are an *employee*. Employees are people who work for the employer. You don't usually use the term 'workers' in business but you often hear the term *workforce* (all the people working in the company). Another very common word for this is *the staff*.
The staff are asking for a safer pension scheme.

▬▬ Note that in American English, you use a singular verb with *staff*. In British English, you use a plural verb.

Pay You *earn* (not *win*) money for the work that you do. The money is your *pay*; pay can be both a noun and a verb. A *wage* is a fixed amount of money, usually paid weekly, often for a job that needs physical strength or skill. A *salary* is a fixed amount of money, agreed every year, and paid to an employee. It's often paid monthly. Your *basic salary* is what you earn before any extra payments. Your *income* is the total amount of money you make in a year, whether you earn it by working or get it in other ways, e.g. by investing or saving.
Most of my employees feel they don't earn enough. My salary is paid directly into my bank account at the end of the month.

Tax When you get paid, your company sends you a *pay slip. Income tax* is a compulsory payment you make to the state if you're employed. If you're not employed but you work, you're *self-employed* and you're responsible for paying your own tax. You have to submit a *tax return* to the government.
My accountant does my tax return because I'm self-employed and it's complicated.

EXTRA TIPS

In the UK, many employed people are on PAYE (Pay As You Earn). This means that the employer takes the income tax and *National Insurance* out of your salary before giving it to you. National Insurance is a compulsory payment which both you and your employer pay. It provides state help to people who are ill, unemployed or retired.

Benefits and pay rises If you feel you're not earning enough, you ask for a *pay rise* (a *raise* in American English). If you get one, it results in a *salary increase*. Many companies also have an annual *salary review*, when they check that every employee's salary is appropriate (usually in response to inflation). You may get *perks*. A perk is a free benefit that the company gives you, e.g. a mobile phone, gym membership. You often join a *pension scheme*. This is a financial plan you and your employer pay into over several years. The money is invested and you benefit from it when you retire.
One of the perks of my job is that I'm able to travel a lot.
Have you joined the company pension scheme?

In some organizations, there are ways of increasing what you earn by *performance-related pay* (an extra payment based on meeting targets), *commission* (payment to people in sales which is a percentage of everything they sell), or a *bonus* (an extra payment sometimes linked to performance or sometimes given to the whole workforce to say thank you).
All our sales reps work on commission. Lucas got a bonus last month.

Giving opinions

Test it ✔

❶ Find and correct **eight mistakes in the sentences**.

~~I'm thinking~~ that your ideas are good.   ..I think....

a   In his manager's opinion, James isn't quite ready for promotion.   ....

b   It's sure that we need to improve our market share.   ....

c   If you ask to me, we need to bring the launch date forward.   ....

d   I think that most people will own a PC by the year 2015.   ....

e   I think that it's not a good idea.   ....

f   To my point of view, delivery dates are the biggest problem.   ....

g   According Leo, we have strong competition in China.   ....

h   Like I see it, we can't continue using these suppliers.   ....

i   We're thinking of taking on some new staff.   ....

j   To my opinion, we've made a lot of progress.   ....

k   To my mind, we need to cut down on our costs before we agree
      to a pay rise.   ....

l   According to me, our logo looks rather old-fashioned.   ....

❷ Look at the sentences. Match the words in bold to their meanings.

a   **I would say that** growth of eight per cent is possible.   ...1...

b   **I guess that** it's time to order some more stationery.   ....

c   **There's no doubt that** the market is very slow at the moment.   ....

d   **Obviously**, we can't agree to a price rise.   ....

e   **As far as we're concerned**, we can't make any changes to the contract.   ....

f   **I'd have thought that** a team of twenty would be OK.   ....

g   **Of course**, we need an innovative marketing campaign.   ....

h   **There's no question that** our profits are disappointing.   ....

1   an opinion you are unsure of (x 2)
2   a strong opinion (x 2)
3   an opinion with which you expect agreement (x 2)
4   an opinion which is likely to be different from other people's
5   an informal opinion

GO to page 48 and check your answers.

Test it again ✔

1 **Find and correct ten mistakes in the dialogue.**

GREG	OK, so what are your thoughts on the new project?	✓ ....
LIZ	~~In~~ my mind, the schedule looks OK.	*To* ....
JOE	Well, at my point view, the production dates are very tight.	....
VICKY	According to me, we can keep the machines running over the weekends if necessary.	....
GREG	I've thought we can complete the order without overtime.	....
JOE	Sorry, there's not doubt that we'll need to do overtime.	....
GREG	OK. I'm guessing that you're right. Let's wait and see.	....
JOE	But I think that isn't an option. We need to plan it now.	....
VICKY	Greg's right. I'm thinking that we need to add overtime costs to the budget now.	....
LIZ	Yes. If you asked me, the budget is unrealistic as it stands.	....
GREG	Right – more money for the budget. It's sure that we agree on that. So, let's get started. As I'm seeing it, the sooner we start, the sooner we get the project finished.	....

2 **True or false?**

		True	False
	'In my opinion technology is the future.' 'I think that technology is the future.' Both these sentences express an opinion.	✓	☐
a	'Of course, we can't ask the staff to accept a pay freeze.' 'Obviously, we can't ask the staff to accept a pay freeze.' In both these sentences, the speaker expects agreement.	☐	☐
b	'As far as we're concerned, the matter is closed.' The speaker may expect other people to disagree.	☐	☐
c	'There's no doubt that we need to close the factory.' 'I'd have said that we need to close the factory.' Both these sentences express a strong opinion.	☐	☐
d	'I guess we have to rethink the situation.' The speaker is talking in formal situation.	☐	☐
e	'We're thinking of opening a new branch.' The speaker is describing an option.	☐	☐
f	'It's obvious that we need to review the contract.' 'It's clear that we need to review the contract.' These sentences have the same meaning.	☐	☐

Answers to Test it

Check your answers. Wrong answer?
Read the right Fix it note to find out why.

1. • ~~I'm thinking~~ I think → B
   a correct → D
   b ~~It's sure~~
      It's clear/I'm sure → F
   c ~~ask to me~~ ask me → A
   d correct → A
   e ~~think that it's not~~
      don't think (that) it's → C
   f ~~To~~ From → D
   g ~~According~~ According to → E
   h ~~Like~~ As → D
   i correct → B
   j ~~To~~ In → D
   k correct → D
   l ~~According to me~~
      I think/In my opinion *etc.* → E

2. a 1 → F   e 4 → G
   b 5 → A   f 1 → F
   c 2 → F   g 3 → G
   d 3 → G   h 2 → F

Now go to page 49. Test yourself again.

Answers to Test it again

1. a ~~at my point view~~
      from my point of view
   b ~~According to me~~
      I think/In my opinion *etc.*
   c ~~I've thought~~ I'd have thought
   d ~~not doubt~~ no doubt
   e ~~I'm guessing~~ I guess
   f ~~think that isn't~~ don't think that's
   g ~~I'm thinking~~ I think
   h ~~asked me~~ ask me
   i ~~It's sure~~ It's obvious/clear
   j ~~I'm seeing~~ I see

2. a True   d False
   b True   e True
   c False   f True

Fix it notes

A Use *I think* (*that*) to express an opinion. *I guess* (*that*) is more informal. You can also use *if you ask me, ...* to introduce an opinion.

B *I think* (*that*) in the present simple means 'I believe'. *I'm thinking of* + *-ing* form in the present continuous means 'I have the idea ...'.

C It's more common to make the 'thinking' verb negative to express a negative opinion, e.g. *I don't think it's a good idea* (not *I think it's not a good idea*).

D Use the expressions *in my opinion/ view, to my mind/way of thinking, from my point of view, as I see it* to give opinions.

E Use *according to* + person to give another person's opinion. You can't say *according to me*. Use *I think* or a phrase from note D.

F To express an opinion in a strong way, use *there's no question/doubt* (*that*) ... or *it's obvious/clear* (*that*) (not *it's sure that*). To express an opinion in a tentative way, use *I'd have thought* (*that*) or *I would think/say* (*that*).

G You can introduce an opinion with *of course* or *obviously* when you expect agreement. You can use *as far as I'm concerned* when your opinion is different from other people's.

For more information, see the Review page opposite.

ℹ Review

Giving opinions You use *I think* (*that*) to express an opinion. *I guess* (*that*) is more informal. You can also use *if you ask me, ...* to introduce an opinion.
I think that it's time to expand.
If you ask me, the conference was a waste of time.

You can also use the following expressions to give opinions:
in my opinion/view, to my mind/my way of thinking, from my point of view, as I see it.
In my view, we need to improve our public image.
As I see it, we can cut production costs.

Simple vs continuous *I think* (*that*) in the present simple means 'I believe'. *I'm thinking of* + -*ing* form in the present continuous means 'I have the idea ...'.
We think that we can do business with this company. (= an opinion)
We're thinking of doing business with this company. (= a possible plan)

Negative forms It's more common to make the 'thinking' verb negative to express a negative opinion, rather than the second verb.

⚠ *I don't think we'll be ready on time.*
(NOT ~~I think we won't be ready ...~~).

According to You use *according to* + person to give another person's opinion. You can't say *according to me*, so use *I think* or another expression from 'Giving opinions' above.
According to the press, share prices are going to fall.

Strength of opinions To express an opinion in a strong way, you can use *there's no question/doubt* (*that*) or *it's obvious/clear* (*that*) (not *it's sure that*). To express an opinion in a tentative way, you use *I'd have thought* (*that*) or *I would think/say* (*that*).
There's no doubt that this is a great opportunity.
I'd have thought that we could negotiate a better deal.

Shared and different opinions
You introduce an opinion with *of course/obviously* when you expect agreement. Be careful not to overuse these expressions as you may sound arrogant if people don't in fact share your opinion or if they are unaware of the situation you're describing.
Of course, we'll need to invite our competitors to the launch.

You can use *as far as I'm concerned* when your opinion is different from other people's. Note that you can use this phrase in the second and third person singular as well.
As far as we're concerned, the costs are not negotiable.
As far as you're concerned, the expansion will be beneficial.
As far as Joe Smith's concerned, our advertising campaign has failed.

Neutral opinions When you don't have a strong opinion, you can use *I don't mind* or *I'm easy* (informal).
I don't mind what we do.
Sounding impartial When you want to make your opinion sound impartial (unbiased), you can use the passive and phrases such as *it seems, it's clear, likely, evident.* Even when you have a strong personal point of view, you can use the passive or these phrases to make your opinion sound more objective to your listener.
It has been said that your department is under-performing.
It seems that sales will decrease in the first quarter of next year.
It's clear that property prices are starting to decrease.

Meetings

Test it ✓

1 Circle the correct option.

We have a (weekly)/week team meeting to discuss progress.

a I'll send you the agenda/minutes for the meeting so that you know what needs to be discussed.

b Rhona is working at home today so she sends her excuses/apologies.

c What did you decide at the department/departmental meeting?

d Let's decide on the action notes/points before we finish the meeting.

e Would you mind taking the minutes/agenda during the meeting?

f AGM stands for 'Annual General/Global Meeting'.

g AOB stands for 'any other briefing/business'.

2 Replace the words in bold with the words below.

miss   close   attend   hold   set up   chair   circulate   ~~draw up~~

Can you **prepare** the agenda for the team meeting?   *draw up*

a Have you **arranged** the team meeting for next month?   ....

b How many people are going to **come to** the meeting?   ....

c Can I ask you to **lead** the meeting?   ....

d Don't forget to **send out** the minutes of the meeting.   ....

e Where do you want to **have** the AGM?   ....

f Can I **finish** the meeting by thanking you all for your contribution?   ....

g If you **don't come to** the meeting, it will be difficult for you to deal with the clients.   ....

3 Find and correct the mistake in each sentence.

Shall I ~~write~~ the minutes this week?   *take*

a 'Where's the planning meeting?' 'To Joe's office.'   ....

b I'm meeting to new clients tomorrow morning.   ....

c It's important for us to finish on time to send out the revised figures. ....

d We were going to finish the meeting at 1 p.m. but we ran on time.   ....

e We're meeting today on 3 p.m.   ....

f We had a useful meeting in the new product designs.   ....

g Let's move to the next point in the agenda.   ....

h Did you have a meeting the head of marketing?   ....

GO to page 52 and check your answers.

Test it again ✔

❶ Choose the correct words to complete the dialogue.

agenda   chair   action points   apologies   attend
~~departmental~~   miss   circulate   minutes

ANGELA Welcome to today's *departmental.* meeting. It's my turn to
ᵃ........................ the meeting, so I'll try to finish on time. There are
several points on the ᵇ........................, so let's get started. Tim, can I ask
you to take the ᶜ........................ and to ᵈ........................ them after the
meeting.

TIM   Sure. Sorry Angela, but Sally can't ᵉ........................ today because she's
not feeling well. She sends her ᶠ........................ .

ANGELA OK, but it's a shame she's going to ᵍ........................ the meeting –
I wanted to get her ideas for the training programme.

TIM   Well, if there are any ʰ........................ for training at the end of the
meeting, I can handle them.

ANGELA Good. Thanks.

❷ Circle the correct option, A or B.

Why are they ...... the AGM in August when everyone will be on holiday?
A making **(B)** holding

a I'm trying to set ...... a meeting for early next week.
A in **B** up

b Why do our meetings always run ...... time? I'm sick of getting home late.
A over **B** in

c I'd like to ...... the meeting soon as it's getting late.
A shut **B** close

d OK, is there any other ...... to discuss before we finish?
A business **B** businesses

e Why do we need another meeting ...... budgets? We've had so many already.
A for **B** on

f Am I ...... to add some points to the agenda?
A in time **B** on time

g How was your meeting ...... the head of Sales?
A to **B** with

h I haven't ...... up the agenda yet so I can't send it out.
A made **B** drawn

Answers to Test it

Check your answers. Wrong answer?
Read the right Fix it note to find out why.

1 ● weekly → E
  a agenda → A
  b apologies → C
  c departmental → D
  d points → C
  e minutes → A
  f General → D
  g business → A

2 ● draw up → A
  a set up → B
  b attend → B
  c chair → B
  d circulate → A
  e hold → B
  f close → B
  g miss → B

3 ● ~~write~~ take → A
  a ~~To~~ In → E
  b ~~meeting to~~ meeting → D
  c ~~on time~~ in time → E
  d ~~on~~ over → E
  e ~~on~~ at → E
  f ~~in~~ on/about → D
  g ~~in~~ on → A
  h ~~meeting~~ meeting with → D

Now go to page 51. Test yourself again.

Answers to Test it again

1 a chair   e attend
  b agenda   f apologies
  c minutes   g miss
  d circulate   h action points

2 a B   b A   c B   d A
  e B   f A   g B   h B

🔧 Fix it notes

A Use *agenda* to talk about the things to discuss at a meeting. You *draw up* an agenda when you prepare it. Use *AOB* (*any other business*) for things not *on the agenda* that are discussed at the end. You *take minutes* when you write a summary of a meeting. You *circulate* the agenda (before) and the minutes (afterwards).

B You *set up a meeting* when you decide the date and time; you *hold* (have) it at a particular time and place; you *attend* if you go to it and you *miss* it if you don't; you *chair* if you're the person in charge; you *close* it when you say it's over.

C You *send apologies* to say you can't attend. *Action points* are tasks people carry out after a meeting.

D You *meet someone/have a meeting with* someone. A meeting is *on/about* something. Use *departmental meeting* for a meeting of a whole department; use *AGM* (*Annual General Meeting*) for a meeting held every year to discuss issues and elect new officials.

E Use *at* + time to say when a meeting is; use *in* + place to say where it is; use *go/run over time* to say a meeting was longer than planned; *in time* means 'early enough' and *on time* means 'at the right time'. *Weekly* means 'every week'.

For more information, see the Review page opposite.

ⓘ Review

Agenda and minutes You use *agenda* to talk about the agreed list of things that people talk about at a meeting. You *draw up* an agenda when you prepare it. The things listed are called *points* or *items*. You use *AOB* (*any other business*) to refer to things that aren't on the agenda and that are discussed at the end of a meeting.
Ken has drawn up the agenda – there are only five items, so it should be quite quick.
'Do we have any other business?' 'Yes. I'd like to talk about the venue for our away day.'

Minutes are a written summary of a meeting. You *take minutes* when you write notes during a meeting. After the meeting you *write up* the minutes when you write your notes in a form other people will be able to read. You decide on *action points* when you give people different tasks to carry out after a meeting. You *circulate* the agenda before a meeting and the minutes after a meeting. This means that you send the minutes to everyone who was at the meeting and to people who may have been absent but should have been there.
Jen is taking minutes and will circulate them tomorrow.

Verbs You *meet* someone or *have a meeting with* someone. In American English and in spoken British English you will probably hear people say *meet with*.
I'm having a meeting with the Managing Director later today.
I met (with) the new designer yesterday.

You *set up* a meeting when you organize the date and time. You *hold* (have) a meeting at a particular time and place. You *attend* a meeting if you go to it and you *miss* it if you don't.

You *send apologies* to say that you're sorry that you can't attend a meeting. You *chair* a meeting if you're the person in charge of it. The person who chairs a meeting is called the *chair* or *chairperson*. You *close* a meeting when you say that it's over.

Types of meeting You can use other nouns to define the type of meeting you're talking about, e.g. *marketing, scheduling, budget, production meeting.*

You use *departmental meeting* to talk about a meeting of a whole department; you use *AGM* (*Annual General Meeting*) to talk about the meeting held by a business/organization every year to discuss issues and elect new officials.
Our production meeting at 2.00 will clash with the AGM at 2.30.

A meeting is *on/about* a particular subject, e.g. *a meeting on/about training new staff.*

Prepositions You use *at* + time to say when a meeting is; you use *in* + place to say where a meeting is; you use *go/run over time* or *the meeting overran* to say a meeting was longer than planned; you use *in time* to mean 'early enough' and *on time* to mean 'at exactly the right time.'
We finished the meeting on time. (at the scheduled time)
We finished the meeting in time to send out the new schedule. (early enough to send out the new schedule)
The meeting overran so I was late for the next one. (It went on longer than planned.)

Frequency You add *-ly* to *week/fortnight/month* to mean 'every week/fortnight/month'.
We have a weekly production meeting.

EXTRA TIPS

Note that you often use the following phrases in meetings:
I agree/disagree (with) ...
I do/don't agree (with) ...
I (don't) think so ...
What about ...?
How about ...?
Why don't I/you/we ...?
Let's ...
As far as I'm concerned ...

Numbers and figures

Test it ✔

1 **How do you say the numbers in these sentences? Circle the correct option, A or B.**

Inflation is at 0 for the third successive quarter.
A oh **B** zero

a We launched the original product in 2006.
A twenty hundred and six   **B** two thousand and six

b We need to add 2,000m² to the measurement.
A two thousand squared metres   **B** two thousand square metres

c Can we decrease it by 2/3?
A two threes   **B** two thirds

d The staff voted for the new system by a ratio of 2:1.
A two to one   **B** two by one

e Profits have dropped to 12%.
A twelve percentage   **B** twelve per cent

f The new screen measures just 15.5cm.
A fifteen point five   **B** fifteen comma five

g We're working on a price of $2.50.
A two dollars fifty   **B** two dollars and fifty

h We need 500GB of memory.
A five hundred gigabytes   **B** five hundreds of gigabytes

i The business needs to operate 24/7.
A twenty-four out of seven   **B** twenty-four seven

j Can you increase the length by 0.5mm?
A nought point five   **B** oh point five

2 **Complete the sentences with the correct preposition.**

by   on   in   at   of   from   off   ~~to~~   out of

What's the exchange rate of the euro ...*to*.......... the dollar?

a Seven people .... ten said they would buy the new shampoo.

b .... average adults spend 70 minutes commuting each day.

c Our profits have risen .... 5%. That's 1.5% higher than forecast.

d If you order today, you can get €200 .... the advertised price.

e If we price the books .... $5, I'm sure we'll get better sales.

f How do you explain the increase .... price?

g We need to increase market share .... 20% to 30%.

h What's the current rate .... interest on our business loan?

GO to page 56 and check your answers.

Test it again ✓

❶ Match a–i and 1–9

a How big was the majority of shareholders backing him?	**1** 24/7.	**a** ..2....
b What's the ratio of men to women in your company?	**2** 2/3.	**b** ....
c What's the measurement of the new site?	**3** $1.210.	**c** ....
d How much memory do you think we need to supply?	**4** Only about 8%.	**d** ....
e What was the main result of the product trial?	**5** Another 20GB.	**e** ....
f What's the rate of exchange of the euro to the US dollar?	**6** Let's say a discount of 5%.	**f** ....
g What percentage of people over 30 use our products?	**7** 2:1.	**g** ....
h How much could you take off for a big order?	**8** 50,000 m^2.	**h** ....
i How many hours will we need to work to meet the deadline?	**9** Only two out of ten people said they would use it.	**i** ....

❷ Find and correct ten mistakes in the presentation.

> **I'D LIKE TO GIVE YOU SOME RESULTS FROM OUR STAFF SURVEY.**
>
> ■ Only 503 ~~out~~ *of* the 1000 of employees we interviewed said they had job satisfaction.
>
> ■ The other fifty percentage said they felt stressed and undervalued.
>
> ■ We're losing employees at a rate off three a month for average and the ratio of men to women in management is five by one.
>
> **BOTH OF THESE SITUATIONS NEED URGENT ACTION.**
>
> ■ We've also experienced an increase at strike action and profits have fallen for 12.9% over the last year.
>
> ■ We need to improve staff morale at the current satisfaction level of just half up something nearer three quarter in the coming year.

⊕ Fix it

Answers to Test it

Check your answers. Wrong answer?
Read the right Fix it note to find out why.

1 ● B → A   f A → A
  a B → C   g A → C
  b B → B   h A → B
  c B → A   i B → C
  d A → A   j A → A
  e B → A

2 ● to   → D
  a out of → E
  b On   → E
  c by   → D
  d off   → D
  e at   → F
  f in   → F
  g from   → F
  h of   → D

Now go to page 55. Test yourself again.

Answers to Test it again

1 a 2   d 5   g 4
  b 7   e 9   h 6
  c 8   f 3   i 1

2 a ~~1,000 of employees~~
    1,000 employees
  b ~~fifty percentage~~   fifty percent
  c ~~rate off three a month~~
    rate of three a month
  d ~~for average~~   on average
  e ~~five by one~~   five to one
  f ~~increase at strike action~~
    increase in strike action
  g ~~for 12.9%~~   by 12.9%
  h ~~at the current satisfaction level~~
    from the current satisfaction level
  i ~~up something nearer~~
    to something nearer
  j ~~three quarter~~   three quarters

⊕ Fix it notes

A Use *half, third, quarter*, etc. in fractions. Use *two to one* etc. to express a ratio (2:1 etc.). Use *per cent* when you want to say the symbol %; the noun is *percentage*. Use *point* when saying a decimal number. Use *nought* or *zero* for 0.

B Use *square* in measurements of areas. Don't use *of* with a whole number and units of measurement (*gigabyte, kilo*, etc.). Don't add *-s* to *hundred/thousand* in exact numbers.

C Read dates beginning 200- as *two thousand and* ... Don't use *and* in prices unless you also use *pence, cents*, etc. Use *twenty-four seven* (24/7) to refer to something that happens twenty-four hours a day, seven days a week.

D Use *rate + to* ask about currency, e.g. *What's the yen exchange rate to the dollar?* Use *rate + of* with words like *interest, unemployment, inflation*. Use *by* to say how big a change is. Use *off* to refer to a discount.

E Use *out of* to say how many people in a group you are talking about, e.g. *six out of ten*. Use *on average* to talk about what is typical of a group of people or things.

F Use *price at* to decide/display the price of something. Use *increase + in* to talk about a rise in something. Use *increase + from ... to* to specify a change of numbers.

For more information, see the Review page opposite.

i Review

Fractions You use *half, third, quarter*, etc. in fractions. You use *two to one* etc. to express a ratio. You use *per cent* when you want to say the symbol %; the noun is *percentage*. You use *point* when saying a decimal number, e.g. 1.5 = *one point five*.
Three quarters of consumers are in debt.
The ratio of staff to managers is 10:1.
What percentage profit are you expecting?

Use *nought* or *zero* for 0 in figures and *'oh'* for 0 in telephone numbers. Note that *nought* is generally a British English word. In American English, you say *zero*.

Measurements You use *square* in measurements of areas, e.g. *100 square metres*.

Don't use *of* with a whole number and units of measurement (*gigabyte, kilo, volt*, etc.)
It's using 500 gigabytes. NOT ~~...500 of gigabytes~~
They airfreighted 2000 kilos of merchandise last week. NOT ~~...2000 of kilos of merchandise~~

You don't add *-s* to hundred/thousand in exact numbers.
Ten thousand people have signed up to our website. BUT *Thousands of customers are switching gas supplier every day.*

Dates and times You read dates beginning 200- as *two thousand and ...*, e.g. 2009 = *two thousand and nine*. For dates from 2010 onwards (2010, 2015, etc.), you say *twenty ten, twenty fifteen*, etc.

🇺🇸 In American English you can say *two thousand nine* or *two thousand and nine* for 2009.

You use *twenty-four seven* to refer to something that happens twenty-four hours a day, seven days a week or to mean 'all the time'.
As the CEO, I have to be on call 24/7.

Costs and prices You don't use *and* in prices unless you use the word *pence/cents*, e.g. £70.24 = *seventy pounds twenty-four* or *seventy pounds and twenty-four pence*.

You use *rate + to* to ask about currency. You use *rate + of* with words like *interest, unemployment, inflation*, etc.
What's the yen exchange rate to the dollar?
What's the current rate of inflation?

You use *price at* to decide/display the price of something. Use *off* to refer to a discount.
We've priced the new computer at $149.99.
We got a discount off the advertised price.

Changes in numbers You use *by* to say how big a change is.
Costs have fallen by a third.

You use *out of* to say how many people in a group you are talking about.
Six out of ten managers said they had recruitment problems.

You use *on average* to talk about what is typical of a group of people or things.
On average, people work a seven-hour day.

You use *increase + in* to talk about a rise in something. You use *increase + from ... to* to specify a change of numbers.
There's been an increase in gas costs.
There's been an increase in costs from 12% to 15%.

A *sharp* increase is big and quick; the opposite is a *slight* increase. The negative of increase is *decrease*. You can also talk about a *rise* (increase) and *fall* (decrease).
There's been a sharp rise in commercial mortgage rates this tax year.

When you talk about patterns in figures, you can talk about them as *trends*.
Recent trends suggest that interest rates will fall.

EXTRA TIPS

Collections of data that are presented to the public (as graphs, charts, etc.) are often called *indices*. The singular is *index*, e.g. *consumer price index, 100 share index*.
The FTSE100 share index fell to 5996 points.

If something grows or increases *exponentially*, its growth/increase becomes faster and faster.
House prices in the UK increased exponentially between 1999 and 2003.

The phone

Test it ✓

1 Find and correct the mistake in each dialogue.

	TIM	Hi, can I speak to Rachel, please?	✓ ....
	RACHEL	~~Talking~~.	.Speaking....
a	RECEPTIONIST	Good morning. AM Designs.	....
	LEO	Hello. Can you put me through the production	....
		department?	....
b	EDDIE	Angela, this line is very bad. Can you speak on a bit?	....
	ANGELA	OK. Can you hear me now?	....
c	RECEPTIONIST	Can I ask who's calling, please?	....
	MR CLARKE	I'm Jim Clarke.	....
d	FRANK	Can I have extension 4123, please?	....
	RECEPTIONIST	Yes, keep the line, please.	....
e	MR MITCHELL	Can you hear me? I'm on my mobile but the sign	....
		isn't very good.	....
	MS EVANS	No, I can't hear you very well.	....
f	SARAH	I need to do a phone call.	....
	DAN	No problem. Use my mobile if you like.	....
g	BEN	Kim isn't in the office at the moment. Would you	....
		like to take a message?	....
	MR LEE	No, thanks. I'll call back later.	....
h	SIMON	Hello, Phil, how are you?	....
	PHIL	Sorry, I'm on the train. I'll make you a ring later.	....

2 Circle the correct option, A or B.

	I'll give you a .... after the meeting.	**A**	phone	**B**	ring
a	Please .... me on my mobile later.	**A**	call	**B**	call to
b	I'm afraid Jo's line is .... Please call back.	**A**	full	**B**	engaged
c	If I give you a .... tomorrow, will you be in?	**A**	calling	**B**	call
d	Why don't you ring them .... if you need them?	**A**	up	**B**	on
e	I called a few times, but I couldn't get	**A**	through	**B**	to
f	Sorry, I didn't .... that. Can you repeat it?	**A**	hold	**B**	catch
g	Oh no, I think I .... the wrong number.	**A**	directed	**B**	dialled
h	Do you know the .... for Spain?	**A**	code	**B**	prefix
i	I've moved offices. I'm on .... 4123 now.	**A**	number	**B**	extension
j	Can you put me .... to Ann, please?	**A**	on	**B**	through

GO to page 60 and check your answers.

Test it again ✅

1 Circle the correct option.

DEBRA   Hello, can you put me through **to**/by Danny Shaw, please?

RECEPTIONIST   One moment, please ... I'm afraid his ᵃline/signal is engaged.

DEBRA   OK, could you try Helen Walker, please?

RECEPTIONIST   Of course. ᵇDial/Hold the line, please.

HELEN   Hello.

DEBRA   ᶜAre you/Is that Helen?

HELEN   Yes, ᵈhere/speaking.

DEBRA   Oh hi, Helen. It's Debra. I tried your mobile a few times yesterday, but I couldn't ᵉgo/get through.

HELEN   Yes, I was out of town and the ᶠcode/signal was very bad.

DEBRA   Don't worry. I wanted to give you a ᵍphone/call to arrange a meeting. Can you make Tuesday at 3.30?

HELEN   Sorry, I didn't ʰcatch/find that. Did you say Thursday?

DEBRA   No, Tuesday at 3.30.

HELEN   Yes, that's fine.

2 Find and correct five mistakes in the speech bubbles.

Could you take a message for Linda Rowe?

correct ....

a Did you remember to ring to the printer about the brochures?

....

b Don't forget you need the code for Manchester to call from here.

....

c I can hardly hear you. Can you speak up, please?

....

d You shouldn't make personal calls from the office phone.

....

e I think you've got the wrong number. What number did you make?

....

f Why is her line always occupied? I can never get through.

....

g Give me a ring when you're next in the area.

....

h Hello, I'm Jane here. Is Gary in the office today?

....

i Can you put me through to extended 2197, please?

....

⚙ Fix it

Answers to Test it

Check your answers. Wrong answer?
Read the right Fix it note to find out why.

1. ● ~~Talking~~ Speaking → D
   a ~~through the~~
      through to the   → C
   b ~~on~~   up   → E
   c ~~I'm~~   It's   → D
   d ~~keep~~   hold   → C
   e ~~sign~~   signal   → E
   f ~~do~~   make   → A
   g ~~take~~   leave   → F
   h ~~make~~   give   → A

2. ● B → A   f B → E
   a A → A   g B → B
   b B → C   h A → B
   c B → A   i B → B
   d A → A   j B → C
   e A → C

◀ Now go to page 59. Test yourself again.

Answers to Test it again

1. a line
   b Hold
   c Is that
   d speaking
   e get
   f signal
   g call
   h catch

2. a ~~ring to~~   ring
   b correct
   c correct
   d correct
   e ~~make~~   dial
   f ~~occupied~~   engaged
   g correct
   h ~~I'm~~   it's
   i ~~to extended~~ extension

⚙ Fix it notes

A You *make a phone call* or *give someone a call/a ring*. You *phone/call/ring* someone (not *phone/call/ring to*) and you can also say *ring/phone* someone *up*.

B You *dial* a number when you press the buttons on a phone in order. You need a *code* to call a different city/country. In an office, the number of a particular phone or office is an *extension*.

C If you don't succeed in making a call, you can't *get through*. The line is *engaged/busy*. You ask to be *put through to* the person you want to speak to. You *hold the line* while waiting to be connected.

D When you want to say who you are on the phone, use *it's* + your name. You say *Is that ...?* to ask who you're speaking to, and *'Speaking'* to confirm that you're the person the caller wants to speak to.

E If you want someone to speak more loudly, you ask them to *speak up*. If the *signal* on a mobile is bad/weak, you can't hear the other person clearly. If you didn't understand what the other person said on the phone, use *I didn't catch that*.

F You *take a message* when you take information from a caller and give it to someone else. You *leave a message* when the person you want to speak to isn't there.

For more information, see the Review page opposite. ▷

ⓘ Review

Making calls You *make a phone call* or *give* someone *a call/ring*. You *phone/call/ring* someone (not *phone/call/ring to* someone) and you can also say *ring/phone* someone *up*.
Can I make a call to my secretary, please?

You say that you're *on the phone* when you're talking to someone. You say *call back* to mean 'call again later'.
Could you be quieter? I'm on the phone.
I'm really busy. Can I call you back later?

You *dial a number* when you press the buttons on a phone in order. You need a *code* to call a different city/country. In an office, the number of a particular phone or office is an *extension*.
Is +33 still the code for France?

You ask to be *put through to* the person you want to speak to if you first speak to the receptionist. You *hold the line* while waiting to be connected.
'Could you put me through to Finance?'
'Yes, please hold the line.'

You ask *to speak to* someone if it's a personal phone call.
Hi, Andy. Can I speak to Amy, please?

Problems You say that you've *got the wrong number* if you dial a number that's incorrect.
'Hello. Is that the Hilton Hotel?' 'No, sorry. You've got the wrong number.'

If you don't succeed in making a call, you say you can't *get through* (because the line is *engaged/busy*). This means someone is already talking on the phone. You also say you can't get through if there's a problem with the phone line.
I couldn't get through to the office as the phone lines were down.

If you want someone to speak more loudly, you ask them to *speak up*. If the *signal* is bad/weak, you can't hear the other person clearly. If you didn't understand what the other person said, you can say *I didn't catch that*.
The signal on my mobile's weak. I didn't catch that. Can you repeat it, please?

Saying who you are When you want to say who you are over the phone, use *it's* and your name. You can use *this is* (name) *from* (name of organization) when you make a call and introduce yourself.
Hello, this is Jim Barber from Fineline here. NOT *Hello, I'm Jim Barber ...*

You say *is that* and a person's name to ask who you are speaking to. You say *yes, speaking* to confirm who you are.
'Hello, is that Mr Sanchez?' 'Yes, speaking.'

Messages You *take a message* when you take information from a caller and give it to someone else. You *leave a message* when the person you want to speak to isn't there. You can leave a message on an answer phone or on someone's voicemail. You can also *pass on a message* or *pass a message on* to someone.
I left several messages on your voicemail.
Could you pass on a message to John in Accounts?

EXTRA TIPS

Mobile phones People use *mobile phones* for other things, as well as making calls. You can *text* someone or *send* them *a text message* – a short written message, often in highly abbreviated English.

You have an account from a mobile phone *network* – a private company that rents phone lines/numbers to businesses and personal clients. You talk about a network having *coverage* or *reception* if it works in a certain area.

When travelling, your phone *roams* between foreign networks – other companies that have an arrangement with your phone company to provide you with coverage when abroad.

With many mobile phones you can also connect to the internet and check email.

Marketing

Test it ✓

① Circle the correct option.

How should we promotion/~~promote~~ our new MP3 player?

a 'What brand/model of cola do you drink?' 'Pepsi.'

b I only buy advertised/branded cosmetics. I think you can trust the big names.

c They say that the McDonald's 'M' is one of most recognized logos/slogans in the world.

d The success of advertising hoardings/signs depends on where they're located.

e People often complain when tobacco companies advertise/sponsor sporting events.

f Many companies use an advert/advertising agency which specializes in persuading people to buy certain products.

g I never read the samples/flyers people give me in the street. It's not a good way to advertise.

h The most successful slogans/logos are short and have a clever use of words.

i The company has just produced a new mix/range of children's clothes.

j We're going to launch/brand our new perfume in time for Christmas.

② Choose a word from each box to complete the sentences.

brand   advertising   special   corporate   product   TV   ~~market~~

offer   ~~research~~   endorsement   image   commercial   awareness   campaign

We interviewed a thousand people as part of our _market research_ .

a Footballers, models and singers are often used for ....

b Our .... will include print and website ads.

c We didn't score well in a .... test – very few people recognized our logo.

d Doing work for charity has improved our ....

e We're going to do a thirty second .... to try to reach as many people as possible.

f The phone company included a .... of free talk time when it advertised its new mobile.

GO to page 64 and check your answers.

Test it again ✔

❶ Match a–h and 1–8.

a The campaign was a disaster. Awareness of our
b We asked the England football captain
c We paid a fortune for a TV
d The ads that we used on the hoardings were a disaster –
e We offered to sponsor a horse race
f The agency made a mistake on the special
g There was a lot of damage to our corporate
h The product isn't selling well because our market

1 half of them were upside down!
2 commercial but people just said it was silly.
3 offer and advertised 100 free calls instead of 10.
4 image when the director was sent to prison.
5 research wasn't very accurate.
6 but they said we didn't have a big enough brand name.
7 brand actually went down!
8 to endorse our new boots but he broke his leg!

a _7_ ....   b ....   c ....   d ....
e ....   f ....   g ....   h ....

❷ Find and correct five mistakes in the sentences.

Our ~~slogan~~ looks a bit old-fashioned. Let's go for a new design
and new colours.   _logo_ ....

a They've added a new laptop to their range of computers.   ....

b What do you think is more effective – commercials in newspapers
or on a website?   ....

c Our last advertising campaign led to an increase in sales.   ....

d The promotion for the new sun products starts in good time
for the summer.   ....

e The agency produced a series of interesting advertisings.   ....

f I think a supermarket's own-brand products are as good as
branded products.   ....

g How many hoardings should we print to give to people as they
pass the shop?   ....

h I don't think that tobacco and alcohol companies should endorse
public events.   ....

i A lot of advertising brands use rhyme to make them memorable.   ....

j There was a lot of interest when the company launched the new car.   ....

Fix it

Answers to Test it

Check your answers. Wrong answer?
Read the right Fix it note to find out why.

1
- promote → A
  - a brand → B
  - b branded → B
  - c logos → C
  - d hoardings → D
  - e sponsor → E
  - f advertising → A
  - g flyers → D
  - h slogans → C
  - i range → B
  - j launch → B

2
- market research → F
  - a product endorsement → E
  - b advertising campaign → A
  - c brand awareness → B
  - d corporate image → F
  - e TV commercial → A
  - f special offer → F

Now go to page 63. Test yourself again.

Answers to Test it again

1
a 7	e 6
b 8	f 3
c 2	g 4
d 1	h 5

2
- a correct
- b ~~commercials~~
  ads/adverts/ advertisements
- c correct
- d correct
- e ~~advertisings~~
  ads/adverts/ advertisements
- f correct
- g ~~hoardings~~   flyers
- h ~~endorse~~   sponsor
- i ~~brands~~   slogans
- j correct

Fix it notes

A To *promote* a product is to attract
attention to it (noun = *promotion*).
To *advertise* is to put information in
print, on TV, etc. to persuade people
to buy something (noun =
advertisement/ad/advert). An
advertising agency makes adverts;
an *advertising campaign* is a
planned series of adverts and
events. A TV/radio ad can be called
a *commercial*.

B You *launch* a product when you
start selling it. Use *brand* for a
product that is recognized by its
name. *Brand awareness* is the level
of recognition of a brand. *Branded*
products have a *brand name*. Use
range for a company's products of a
particular type.

C A *logo* is a symbol/image used to
represent a company; a *slogan* is a
phrase used to advertise a product.

D *Hoardings* are large adverts used in
public areas; *flyers* are pieces of
paper used to advertise things.

E If a company *sponsors* an event, it
pays some of the costs. *Product
endorsement* is when famous
people recommend a product.

F *Market research* is collecting
information about what people want.
Use *corporate image* to talk about
how a company is seen; a *special
offer* is an extra benefit.

For more information, see the
Review page opposite.

ⓘ Review

Advertising To *promote* a product is to attract people's attention to it. The noun is *promotion*.
A team of 35 is dedicated to promoting our products.
Our Christmas promotions will start on 17 October.

To *advertise* is to put information in print, on TV, etc. to persuade people to buy something. The noun is *advertisement* (also *ad* or *advert*).
How are we going to advertise our new products?
People are exposed to hundreds of adverts a day.

An *advertising agency* specializes in making adverts; an *advertising campaign* is a planned series of adverts and events. Note that you don't shorten the word *advertising* to *advert*, although you can say *ad agency* and *ad campaign*.
We used an advertising agency for our most recent campaign.

An advert on TV or radio is sometimes called a *commercial*.
We can reach millions of people with commercials on TV and radio.

Techniques You use *hoardings* (American English: *billboard*) to talk about large adverts in busy public areas.
We've got our ads on hoardings all over the city.

You use *flyers* to talk about pieces of paper used to advertise something, often given to people in the street.
We've got 500 flyers to advertise the new sandwich shop on the high street.

Products and brands *Market research* is the process of collecting information about what people like to buy.
Our latest market research points to increasing use of our products by women aged 45–60.

You *launch* a product when you start selling it to the public.
Since we launched our new SpeedPlayer, our share price has gone up by 24%.

You use *brand* to talk about a product that can be recognized by its name, e.g. *Coke*, *Niko*. *Brand awareness* is the level of recognition of a brand. *Branded* products have a brand name, e.g. *Chanel*; *own-brand* products are made by the shop that sells them.
Companies want to increase their brand awareness among teenagers.
I don't buy supermarket own-brand tea.

You use *range* to talk about a company's products of a particular type.
They've added watches to their range of jewellery.

Logos and slogans You use *logo* to talk about a symbol or image used to represent a company.
Our logo symbolizes quality and value.

You use *slogan* to talk about a phrase used to advertise a product.
We need a new slogan – the shorter the better.

Company image If a company *sponsors* an event, it pays some of the costs, e.g. of a concert or a race.
Tobacco companies often sponsor Formula 1 racing.

Product endorsement is when famous people recommend a product.
Footballers are often used for product endorsement of sunglasses and clothes.

You use *corporate image* to talk about how a company is seen by the public.
Using only organic ingredients has improved our corporate image.

A *special offer* is an additional benefit used to attract customers, e.g. a free gift or a discount.
Special offer: buy two, get one free.

Time

Test it ✔

❶ Circle the correct option.

We're working on a three-month time/schedule on this project.

a I have to warn you that the schedule is very narrow/tight.

b The deadline/lifeline for this stage of the project is 22 July.

c We can save/waste some time if we check the designs in-house.

d Next Monday will be too late – we need to be ready by/to Friday at the latest.

e We spend/pass hours discussing the same problems.

f Please check the wall calendar/diary to see when staff are taking holidays.

g It was three day's/days' work to finish the project.

h I didn't have lunch today. I was too tight/short of time.

❷ Find and correct five mistakes in the sentences.

The whole team is ~~making~~ overtime this month. ..*doing*..............

a I work really long hours but I'm always short of time. ....

b Good news! The project is behind schedule. ....

c We can't miss time on this project. Time is money. ....

d The models need to be ready until next Friday. ....

e We mustn't get behind schedule on this project. ....

f I'm afraid I don't got time to check your work. ....

g We need to schedule this project immediately. ....

h The clients won't pay us if we lose the deadline. ....

❸ Match a–f and 1–6.

a Why are you wasting time **1** need to get back on track. **a** *6*.

b We've got a big order, **2** we could make the delivery dates. **b** ....

c If we don't deliver on time, **3** completely on schedule! **c** ....

d I don't believe it! This project is **4** so can you do some overtime? **d** ....

e If the staff gave up their holiday, **5** we won't get any future orders. **e** ....

f Why has this schedule slipped? We **6** chatting on the phone? **f** ....

GO to page 68 and check your answers.

Test it again ✔

❶ **Find and correct ten mistakes in the memo.**

MEMO

FROM	Jay Moreland
TO	Production Department
SUBJECT	Scheduling and deadlines

It's clear from our team meeting ~~by~~ *on* Friday that we are seriously on schedule on the Christmas gifts project. I'm not sure why the schedule has fallen so badly but we must miss all the new deadlines in October and November. I'm asking everyone in the department to make overtime so that we can get things back on path. I'll send you revised schedules on the end of this week. Please write all key dates in your desk calendar and check it every week. We're going to work to a very small schedule, so please do not pass any time on work that is not for this project. If we do the new delivery dates, there will be a Christmas bonus for the whole team.

❷ **True or false?**

	TRUE	FALSE
If the schedule slips, it's a good thing.	☐	✔
a It's good to be 'on schedule' or 'on track'.	☐	☐
b You can say 'miss a deadline' or 'lose a deadline'.	☐	☐
c It's better to 'waste time' than to 'spend time'.	☐	☐
d 'Schedule' is a noun and a verb.	☐	☐
e 'I'm short of time' and 'I don't have enough time' mean the same thing.	☐	☐
f The punctuation in 'a months research' isn't correct.	☐	☐

Fix it

Answers to Test it

Check your answers. Wrong answer?
Read the right Fix it note to find out why.

1 • schedule → A   e spend → D
   a tight → A   f calendar → E
   b deadline → B   g days' → F
   c save → D   h short → D
   d by → C

2 • ~~making~~ doing → D
   a correct → D
   b ~~behind~~ on/ahead of → C
   c ~~miss~~ waste/lose → D
   d ~~until~~ by → C
   e correct → C
   f ~~don't got~~ don't have/
       haven't got → D
   g correct → A
   h ~~lose~~ miss → B

3 a 6 → D   d 3 → C
   b 4 → D   e 2 → B
   c 5 → C   f 1 → C

Now go to page 67. Test yourself again.

Answers to Test it again

1 a ~~on schedule~~ behind schedule
   b ~~fallen~~ slipped
   c ~~miss all the new deadlines~~
      meet all the new deadlines
   d ~~make overtime~~ do overtime
   e ~~back on path~~ back on track
   f ~~on the end of this week~~
      by/at the end of this week
   g ~~desk calendar~~ desk diary
   h ~~small schedule~~ tight schedule
   i ~~do not pass any time~~
      do not waste/spend any time
   j ~~do the new delivery dates~~
      make the new delivery dates

2 a True   d True
   b False   e True
   c False   f True

Fix it notes

A Use *schedule* to refer to a plan of activities and when they will happen; use *tight schedule* to say that there's a lot to do in a short time; you can also use *schedule* as a verb.

B Use *deadline* to refer to a time or date by which you have to do something; you *meet a deadline* or *make a date/the dates* if you complete the work by the date and *miss the deadline* if you don't.

C Use *by* for 'not later than'; use *on* with a particular day. Use *on schedule/on time* for 'happening at the planned time', and *behind schedule/the schedule has slipped* for 'late'. Use *get behind schedule* for becoming late and *get back on track* to mean 'get back to the planned schedule'.

D You can say *I've got time* or *I don't have/haven't got time* to do something. You're *short of time* if you don't have enough time. You *spend time* doing an activity; time itself *passes*. You *waste time* if you don't work productively; you *save time* if you use less time than planned. You *do overtime* if you work more than your usual hours.

E A *calendar* is a set of pages showing dates; a *diary* is a book where you write appointments.

F Use *'s/s'* with periods of time, e.g. *a week's work; three weeks' work*.

For more information, see the
Review page opposite.

ⓘ Review

Schedules You use *schedule* to refer to a plan of activities and when they will happen. You use the collocation *tight schedule* to say that there is a lot to do in a short time. You can also use *schedule* as a verb.
There isn't much time left in the schedule.
We're on an incredibly tight schedule so we need to start now.
We scheduled the building of the new office last week.

You use *get behind schedule* to talk about the process of becoming late and *get back on track* to mean 'get back to the planned schedule'.
It's important not to be behind schedule.
How can we get back on track?

Note that you may also hear the word *timetable* used as a noun and a verb instead of *schedule*, but this is not common in a business context.

If something happens and you have to change the schedule, you *update* it, and you can *build* something *into* the schedule.
We'll have to build the new safety tests into the schedule.
I've updated the schedule because of Max's illness.

Deadlines You use *deadline* to refer to a time or date by which you have to do something; you *meet a deadline* or *make a date/the dates/the deadline* if you complete the work by the date and *miss the deadline* if you don't.
Well done! You've met all your deadlines.
What's happens if we miss the deadline?
Can we make the date for delivery?

Prepositions You use *by* to mean 'not later than', often with the expression *at the latest*; *on* refers to a particular day.
Please send me the information by Friday at the latest.
We're opening the new store on Monday.

You use *on schedule* or *on time* to mean 'happening at the planned time', and *behind schedule* or *the schedule has slipped* to mean 'late'.

This stage is on schedule.
We need to deliver on time.
We're behind schedule on the marketing plan.
The schedule has slipped by 10 days.

's or s' You use *'s/s'* with periods of time. Compare:
a day's work (singular)
four days' work (plural).

Verb + time You can say *I have/'ve got* or *I don't have/haven't got time* to do something. You are *short of time* if you don't have enough time.
Do you have time to look at this report?
I'm short of time. I won't be able to attend the meeting.

You *spend time* doing an activity and time itself *passes*; you *waste time* if you don't work productively; you *save time* if you use less time than planned; you *lose time* if you get behind (schedule) but it's no-one's fault, or it's because of circumstances that are beyond your control.
We spent a day planning the presentation.
Time passes quickly when you're busy.
Don't waste time chatting – we need to finish these reports.
We'll save time if we plan everything in advance.
We lost a day due to the postal strike.

Overtime You *do overtime* if you work more than your usual hours.
Can you do overtime at the weekend?

Calendar or diary? You use *calendar* to talk about a set of pages showing dates and *diary* to talk about a book where you write appointments etc.
The key dates are all on the calendar.
Please also write them in your diary.

🇺🇸 In American English, you use the word *calendar* for both words.
Take a look at the calendar and see what day of the week July 10 is.
I'll put the meeting in my calendar so I don't forget it.

Business travel

Test it ✔

❶ Circle the correct option.

There was so much traffic on the roads that I lost/(missed) the flight.

a The hotel bill/fare will be paid by my company.

b We did/made a reservation for twenty delegates at the conference.

c I go on about thirty business trips/travels a year.

d The baggage handlers were on strike/delay so I couldn't get my cases.

e Let's take/go a taxi to the meeting.

f The plane lands/takes off at 7.00 so we'll meet you at the terminal at 7.30.

g I only have a tourist visa/passport so I can't stay longer than ninety days.

h The hotel is always busy in August so you'll need to book/reserve.

i My flight to Milan was stopped/cancelled, so I was late for the meeting.

j Flight BA129 to Helsinki is now boarding/catching through gate 41.

❷ Choose a word from each box to complete the sentences.

> arrivals   passport   final   departure   flight   ~~taxi~~
> check-in   baggage   hand   boarding   domestic

> allowance   desk   flights   pass   luggage   gate
> call   control   attendants   hall   ~~fare~~

I didn't have enough money left for my ...*taxi fare*........ .

a The .... for this flight is only 30kg.

b I went through .... but they didn't even check my photo.

c I wasn't impressed by the airline's service. The .... were rude.

d I always travel light so I only take .... on a flight.

e A driver will be there to meet you in the .... when you land.

f Your seat number is on your ....

g They've announced the flight. We need to go to the .... now.

h Don't go to terminal 1 – that's for the international flights. The
.... leave from terminal 2.

i This case is too big to go on the plane. Which .... do I need to
go to?

j 'This is the .... for flight BA491 to Berlin. Please go to gate 14
immediately.'

GO to page 72 and check your answers.

Test it again ✔

① **Find and correct twelve mistakes in the dialogue.**

LINDA Excuse me, that's my seat. My boarding ~~ticket~~ says I'm in seat 22C. *pass*

BOB You're right, sorry. I'll move my handbags. ....

LINDA Thanks. It's good to sit down. I lost the flight before this one. ....
My train to the airport was annulled. ....

BOB I had a similar problem on a travel last month. There was a ....
strike on the trains so I had to go taxi from home to the airport. ....
The taxi bill was huge. ....

LINDA What a nightmare! What time do we take off in Milan? ....

BOB It's a two-hour flight so we should be there at about eleven. ....
I've reserved a taxi to the city if you'd like to share it. ....

LINDA Thanks, but my boss is meeting me in the arriving hall. ....

BOB OK, no problem. ....

LINDA I'll need to get through visa control quickly as we have lunch ....
with clients at twelve. ....

BOB You should be OK, as we took up on time. ....

LINDA Yes. Oh, here's the flight assistant at last. I'm thirsty. ....

② **Follow the instructions to find words connected with travel.**

Please go to **checked-in** desk 55	take away two letters	*check-in*
a I don't do much business **traveller**.	take away three letters	....
b Please **take** a reservation for a morning flight to New York.	change one letter	....
c Why are the airport staff on **striker**?	take away one letter	....
d I haven't paid my hotel **pill** yet.	change one letter	....
e That was the final **calling** for our flight.	take away three letters	....
f There was a two-hour **relay** on the flight.	change one letter	....
g Which is the terminal for **domesticated** flights?	take away four letters	....
h What's the **cabbage** allowance on this flight?	change three letters	....
i Have you **cooked** the hotel room yet?	change one letter	....
j Flight IB901 to Madrid is now **hoarding** through gate 12.	change one letter	....

🔧 Fix it

Answers to Test it

Check your answers. Wrong answer?
Read the right Fix it note to find out why.

1 • missed → E   f lands → E
   a bill → B   g visa → B
   b made → C   h book → C
   c trips → A   i cancelled → D
   d strike → D   j boarding → E
   e take → C

2 • taxi fare → B
   a baggage allowance → F
   b passport control → B
   c flight attendants → E
   d hand luggage → F
   e arrivals hall → E
   f boarding pass → F
   g departure gate → E
   h domestic flights → E
   i check-in desk → F
   j final call → E

◀ Now go to page 71. Test yourself again.

Answers to Test it again

1 a ~~handbags~~   hand luggage
   b ~~lost~~   missed
   c ~~annulled~~   cancelled
   d ~~a travel~~   a trip
   e ~~go taxi~~   take a taxi/go by taxi
   f ~~taxi bill~~   taxi fare
   g ~~take off~~   land
   h ~~reserved~~   booked
   i ~~arriving hall~~   arrivals hall
   j ~~visa control~~   passport control
   k ~~took up~~   took off
   l ~~flight assistant~~   flight attendant

2 a travel   f delay
   b make   g domestic
   c strike   h baggage
   d bill   i booked
   e call   j boarding

🔧 Fix it notes

A Use *trip* to talk about short journeys and *business trips*. *Travel* is an uncountable noun and refers to the general activity of travelling.

B Use *fare* for a journey's price; use *bill* for a list of what you owe. A *passport* is the official document needed to travel abroad; a *visa* is a document or mark in a passport that allows you to enter or leave a country. You show your passport and visa at *passport control*.

C You *make a reservation* and *book a hotel, flight, conference room*, etc. You *take a taxi* or *go by taxi*.

D A *strike* is a period when people refuse to work. Use *delay* when something is late. If a flight etc. is *cancelled*, it won't leave.

E You *miss* (not *lose*) a flight if you don't catch it. Use *take off/land* when a plane leaves/arrives. You go through the *departure gate* to leave and the *arrivals hall* to land. A *domestic flight* is within the same country. The *final call* is the last announcement before a flight. If a plane is *boarding*, passengers can get on. *Flight attendants* look after the passengers.

F You take your luggage to the *check-in desk*. The *baggage allowance* is the amount of luggage you can take. A bag you carry with you is *hand luggage*. Your *boarding pass* has your seat number on.

> For more information, see the Review page opposite. ▷

ⓘ Review

Trip, travel and *journey* You use *trip* to talk about short journeys and with *business* (*business trip*). *Travel* is an uncountable noun and refers to the general activity of travelling. You use *journey* to talk about going from one place to another.
How was your business trip?
How much foreign travel do you do?
It was a long journey from the airport.

Money You use *fare* for the money you pay for a journey, e.g. *a taxi fare*; you use *bill* for a list of what you owe, e.g. *hotel bill*. You *pay* or *settle* a bill.
I only just had enough money to settle the restaurant bill.

Documents You use *passport* to talk about the official document with a photo needed to travel abroad; you use *visa* to talk about a document or mark in a passport that allows you to enter or leave a country, or stay for a fixed period. You show your passport and visa at *passport control* (American English: *immigration*).

EXTRA TIPS

There are several types of ticket on planes, trains and buses: a *single* (one way), a *return* (there and back), an *open return* (where you don't have to specify when you're returning), and an *open jaw* (where you fly into one city and out of another). *Economy* (*class*) is the cheapest and most basic type of ticket, *business* (*class*) is more expensive, and *first class* is the most expensive.

Verb + noun You *make a reservation* and *book a hotel, flight, conference room,* etc. You *take a taxi* or *go by taxi*.
My secretary made a reservation for me.
We booked a conference room but the organizers had lost all our details.

Problems You use *strike* to talk about a period when people refuse to work – they are *on strike*. You use *delay* to say that something is late. If a flight, train, etc. is *cancelled*, it will not leave.

There was a delay at the airport. OR
The flight was delayed.
The midday train has been cancelled, so I'm going to take a taxi to the airport.

Air travel You *miss* (not *lose*) a flight if you don't catch it.
We were late so we missed our flight.

You use *take off* when a plane leaves the ground and *land* when it arrives.
We took off an hour late but landed on time, thankfully.

You sit in the *departure lounge* to wait for your flight and you get on a plane at the *departure gate*. When you get off the plane, you *go through customs*, where you have to show your passport, and *declare* if you have anything in your luggage which you must pay tax on. If you have nothing, you can follow signs saying *nothing to declare*. You go through the *arrivals hall* when you land.
Would all remaining passengers please go to departure gate 14?

A *domestic flight* is within the same country. The *final call* is the last announcement that a flight is going to take off. If a plane is *boarding*, it is ready for passengers to go on. You can also say *board a train/ship/flight*.
If companies used trains instead of domestic flights, they'd use less carbon.
This is the final call for flight BA203. This flight is boarding now.
We can't board the train – there's a delay.

Flight attendants are the people who look after passengers. This term refers to both men and women and is preferable to *air hostess/steward/stewardess*.

You take your luggage to the *check-in desk* and they weigh it and check your ticket. The *baggage allowance* is the amount of luggage you are allowed. A bag you carry on to the plane is called *hand luggage*. You get a *boarding pass* with your seat number at the check-in desk.
They'll tell you your baggage allowance at the check-in desk.

Cultural matters

Test it ✔

1 **What cultural points are they talking about?**

dress code   titles   ~~eye contact~~   alcohol   introductions
gender   humour   punctuality   smoking

That candidate didn't look at me once during his interview. .....*eye contact*.....

a We were supposed to start at 9.30 but one had arrived. ....

b I always start my speeches with a few jokes. ....

c I asked them where I could smoke and they were all shocked. ....

d He gave me his business card but we didn't shake hands. ....

e I was going to order a beer but everyone else had water. ....

f We always use first names in our company. ....

g It's amazing the number of older men who call me 'dear'. ....

h I walked in wearing jeans – the others were all in suits. ....

2 **Circle the correct option.**

They're much too (direct)/indirect – they just say exactly what they think.

a I find it hard when people don't make/do eye contact.

b It was very tiring – they talked/spoke business the whole time during dinner.

c Don't forget to bow/nod to the Japanese business people at the conference.

d No one gave their surname/first name and six people were called John!

e Jo is so remote/approachable. You have to make an appointment to see her.

f I've known Sam for years so I'm used to him kissing me on/to the cheek.

g It's best to avoid telling/saying jokes, as humour doesn't always translate.

h Is it black suit/tie for the conference dinner?

3 **Find and correct the mistake in each sentence.**

The invitation doesn't specify a ~~dressing~~ code. .....*dress*.....

a This is Miss Jane. She works in the marketing department. ....

b Do you care if I smoke during lunch? ....

c 'Mrs' and 'Miss' are so old-fashioned. Please call me 'Mr'. ....

d I felt a bit embarrassing when no one laughed at my joke. ....

e Can I present you to the Marketing Director? ....

f You must be Mike. It's Joe Mason. Nice to meet you. ....

g When you first meet someone, shake the hands and smile. ....

h The invitation says 'smartly casual' so we don't need suits. ....

GO to page 76 and check your answers.

Test it again ✔

① **Choose the correct words to complete the email.**

humour   alcohol   first names   embarrassing   business   direct
eye contact   embarrassed   punctual   dress code   ~~introduced~~

> Hi Tim
>
> Thanks for setting up the meeting last week. I know the clients weren't all from Europe, but I was surprised that there were people from so many different cultures, when we ...*introduced*... ourselves! I thought they would all be
> **a** .... , but we started the meeting about half an hour late. As for the **b** .... , some people were wearing suits, some jeans and some national costume! I started my presentation with a bit of **c** .... – perhaps they didn't understand my joke but no one even smiled. I tried to make **d** .... but some of them just stared at me and some looked at the desk.
>
> At lunch everyone introduced themselves, but I couldn't remember when to use **e** .... and I think I offended one or two of the women. It was really **f** .... ! One of the men was really **g** .... and he said that he hated the food. I had decided not to order **h** .... but he wanted some whisky. He also insisted on talking **i** .... when everyone else was just chatting. I was so **j** .... that I couldn't wait for lunch to end.

② **Circle the correct option, A or B.**

Is the dinner ..... tie?
A bow   **(B)** black

a It's fine to ..... your head when you greet the local people.
A shake   **B** nod

b I'm not sure if she's married so just use ..... when you address the letter.
A Mrs   **B** Ms

c I don't think I've ..... you to the head of HR.
A introduced   **B** presented

d I like to be ..... . It's important that my staff can talk to me.
A indirect   **B** approachable

e Do you mind if I ..... ?
A smoking   **B** smoke

f It's illegal to discriminate on the grounds of race or ..... .
A female   **B** gender

g Hello, ... Angela Newton, head of Design. Nice to meet you.
A I'm   **B** it's

h The speaker ..... a joke but no one laughed.
A told   **B** said

Fix it

Answers to Test it

Check your answers. Wrong answer?
Read the right Fix it note to find out why.

1 ● eye contact → F
   a punctuality → F
   b humour → E
   c smoking → B
   d introductions → C
   e alcohol → B
   f titles → D
   g gender → D
   h dress code → A

2 ● direct → E   **e** remote → E
   a make → F   **f** on → C
   b talked → E   **g** telling → E
   c bow → C   **h** tie → A
   d surname → D

3 ● ~~dressing~~   dress → A
   a ~~Miss Jane~~   Jane → D
   b ~~care~~   mind → B
   c ~~Mr~~   Ms → D
   d ~~embarrassing~~   embarrassed → E
   e ~~present~~   introduce → F
   f ~~It's~~   I'm → F
   g ~~shake the hands~~
         shake hands → C
   h ~~smartly~~   smart → A

Now go to page 75. Test yourself again.

Answers to Test it again

1 **a** punctual   **f** embarrassing
   b dress code   **g** direct
   c humour   **h** alcohol
   d eye contact   **i** business
   e first names   **j** embarrassed

2 **a** B   **e** B
   b B   **f** B
   c A   **g** A
   d B   **h** A

Fix it notes

A Use *dress code* to talk about what people wear at work. *Black tie* refers to very formal social occasions. *Smart casual* refers to less formal clothes.

B There are different rules about cigarettes and alcohol in different cultures. Use *Do/Would you mind if I smoke/smoked?* before smoking.

C You *bow* when you bend forwards to show respect. You *nod* when you move your head up and down. You *shake hands* or *kiss* someone *on the cheek*.

D Don't confuse *first names* and *surnames*. If you're not sure which title to use for a woman, say *Ms*. Don't use *Mr/Ms/Mrs/Miss* + first name. Use *gender* to refer to the difference between male and female.

E *Humour* refers to funny things or situations. You *tell* (not *say*) *jokes*. If a joke doesn't work, you are *embarrassed* and the situation is *embarrassing*. If you say what you think, you're *direct*. You can talk to an *approachable* person at any time. The opposite is *remote*. You *talk business* over lunch, dinner, etc.

F If you're on time, you are *punctual* (noun = *punctuality*). Use *introduce* (not *present*) when you want people to know each other. When introducing yourself, say *I'm* … You *make* (not *do*) *eye contact*.

> For more information, see the Review page opposite. ▷

ⓘ Review

Clothes You use *dress code* to talk about what people wear at work. The dress code in offices can be *formal* or *informal*. *Black tie* refers to clothes worn for formal social occasions – for men a black bow tie, white shirt and black suit, and for women, a cocktail dress. *Smart casual* refers to clothes that are less formal, e.g. a shirt and trousers but no tie for men and trousers and a sweater for women.
Only the waiters and I were in black tie, as the dress code was smart casual.

Entertainment There are different rules about smoking and drinking alcohol in different cultures – some find both acceptable, others don't. If you want to smoke, you use *Do you mind if I smoke?/Would you mind if I smoked?* before you light a cigarette, or ask whether the company has a smokers' room.

You can have business lunches, where you *talk business* (discuss business affairs) over lunch. Note that *business* in this sense is an uncountable noun, so you don't use an article.
We started talking business over lunch, and had closed the deal by dessert.

Greetings and introductions In some cultures you *bow* when you bend your body forwards to show respect for someone. You *nod* when you move your head up and down as a way of saying hello. You *shake hands* (not *shake the hands*). You *kiss* someone *on the cheek* if you know them well.

You use the verb *introduce*, not *present*, when you want two people you know to meet each other. When you introduce yourself, you say *I'm …* (not *It's …*). You *make eye contact*; be sensitive to other cultures if they avoid eye contact or don't hold eye contact for long.

Titles and names Don't confuse *first names*, e.g. *Maria*, and *surnames*, e.g. *Jacobson*. Generally you use *Mr/Ms* + surname until you know someone well enough to use first names. If you are not sure which title to use for a woman, always use *Ms*. Don't use *Mr/Ms/Mrs/Miss* + first name, e.g. *Mr John, Ms Karen*.

Political correctness Use *gender* to refer to talk about the difference between male and female, e.g. *gender equality*. Use *sexuality* to refer to someone's sexual preferences, e.g. *gay, straight*. Use *race* to refer to their racial origins (*ethnicity*). If a company treats an employee differently because of any of these things, it's *discrimination*, and if an individual treats another employee differently, it may be *harassment*, e.g. *sexual harassment*. Both are illegal in many cultures, and against employees' rights. Use *political correctness* (adjective: *politically correct*) to talk about treating everyone with respect, sensitivity and tact, regardless of their sex, race, age, sexuality, etc.

Humour *Humour* refers to things or situations that are funny. You *tell* (not *say*) *jokes*. Humour doesn't always translate into other languages, and some things that are funny in one culture may not be funny in another. If a joke doesn't work, you are *embarrassed* and the situation is *embarrassing*.
I told the joke about the monkey and the fries but was embarrassed when no one laughed.

Punctuality If you're on time, you are *punctual*. The noun is *punctuality*. Different cultures have different views on punctuality. For some people it's OK to be a bit late for a meeting but for others it's extremely important to be on time.

Directness If people say exactly what they think, they are *direct*. Although being direct is not the same as being rude, it can seem rude, so be careful. Follow the example of the people you're with.

An *approachable* person is one that you can talk to at any time. If someone isn't approachable, you can say that they're *unapproachable, remote* or *distant*.
It's true that Bob can upset people by being too direct, but he's also a very approachable boss.

Presentations

Test it ✓

1 Write the missing vowels to make nouns and verbs connected with presentations.

n .o. t .e. s

a s l ..... d .....

b g ..... s t ..... r ..... s

c s t ..... g .....

d s p .... k ..... r

e .... d .... n c .....

f s c r .... n

g t ..... l k

h r ..... c ..... p

2 Match a–i to 1–9.

a Power	**1** language	**a** .4.
b flip	**2** card	**b** .....
c eye	**3** show	**c** .....
d cue	**4** Point	**d** .....
e slide	**5** chart	**e** .....
f visual	**6** demo	**f** .....
g body	**7** out	**g** .....
h online	**8** contact	**h** .....
i hand	**9** aids	**i** .....

3 Complete the tips with words from exercise 2 and the words and phrases below.

question and answer session   microphone   OHT   presentation
project   ~~introduction~~   OHP

- Your _introduction_ needs to get the audience's attention. Make ª........................ immediately and use an anecdote or a statistic to start things off.

- Make sure your ᵇ........................ is carefully structured.

- Prepare ᶜ........................ like slides and company products in advance.

- If you're going to use an ᵈ........................, or give a ᵉ........................ presentation, don't forget to check the power supply!

- Check the spelling in every ᶠ........................ . People love pointing out mistakes!

- Your ᵍ........................ is important. Be aware of the way you move.

- Involve your audience. Leave time for a ʰ........................ .

- ⁱ........................ your voice effectively, or use a ʲ........................ .

GO to page 80 and check your answers.

Test it again ✅

1 Find and correct eight mistakes in the presentation.

Good morning, everyone, and thank you for coming. My
presentation
~~presenter~~ today is about new markets in Europe. I'm

going to give a slide showing so I hope you can all see

the audience clearly. There's no need to take slides as

I'll end with an uncap and I'll give you a cue card of

the main points to take away with you. I'll also leave

time for a question and answer period. I'm afraid the

telephone isn't working so I hope you can hear me. I'll

try to protect my voice so that the people at the back

can hear.

2 Circle the correct option.

TRAINER OK, Ellen. Let's have a look at the video of your presentation. You're a quite a confident (speaker)/talker, but you need to plan your **a** presents/talks better. You began with a good **b** introduction/summing up, but then you forgot what you wanted to say.

ELLEN Yes, I couldn't follow my **c** cards/notes and I got lost.

TRAINER I see. One other problem was your writing on the flip **d** chart/board – it was very unclear. Why not put the key points on an **e** OHT/OHP and use the **f** OHP/OHT to display the text?

ELLEN That's a good idea but I'm not very confident with technology.

TRAINER Well, I can give you some training on **g** PowerPlant/PowerPoint presentations and on **h** offline/online demos.

ELLEN Great. Thanks. What about the rest of my presentation?

TRAINER Well, you tended to move around the **i** stage/screen too much, so the **j** crowd/audience got a bit distracted. You also used too many **k** visual/vision aids, which was rather confusing. You are very enthusiastic, but keep your **l** gestures/moves small – don't wave your hands around so much. The rest of your body **m** communication/language is OK but don't forget to make **n** visual/eye contact at all times.

Answers to Test it

Check your answers. Wrong answer?
Read the right Fix it note to find out why.

① • notes → B   e audience → A
  a slide → B   f screen → B
  b gestures → F   g talk → E
  c stage → A   h recap → E
  d speaker → A

② a 4 → C   d 2 → B   g 1 → F
  b 5 → D   e 3 → C   h 6 → C
  c 8 → F   f 9 → D   i 7 → D

③ • introduction → E
  a eye contact → F
  b presentation → E
  c visual aids → D
  d OHP → C
  e PowerPoint → C
  f OHT/slide/handout → C, B, D
  g body language → F
  h question and answer
    session → E
  i Project → F
  j microphone → B

Now go to page 79. Test yourself again.

Answers to Test it again

① a ~~slide showing~~ slide show
  b ~~audience~~ screen/stage
  c ~~slides~~ notes
  d ~~uncap~~ recap
  e ~~cue card~~ handout
  f ~~period~~ session
  g ~~telephone~~ microphone
  h ~~protect~~ project

② a talks   h online
  b introduction i stage
  c notes   j audience
  d chart   k visual
  e OHT   l gestures
  f OHP   m language
  g PowerPoint n eye

🔧 Fix it notes

A A *stage* is the place where you stand to give a presentation. Use *audience* to talk about the people listening to the *speaker*.

B Use *notes* or *cue cards* to help you remember the key points of your presentation. Use a *microphone* to make your voice louder, and a *screen* to show text and images. A *slide* is a piece of film with text that can be projected on to a wall or *screen*.

C *PowerPoint* is a computer program. It gives a *slide show* – text and images on a screen. *OHP* stands for overhead projector and *OHT* for overhead transparency. An *online demo* (demonstration) uses the internet in a presentation.

D A *handout* is a piece of paper or object, e.g. your product, that you give to the audience. A *flip chart* has large sheets of paper for writing or drawing on. A *visual aid* is anything your audience can see.

E A *talk* or *presentation* starts with an *introduction* and ends with a summary or a *recap*. Often the audience participates in a *question and answer session*.

F It's important to *make eye contact* with your audience and to *project* your voice. Your *body language* includes eye contact, *gestures* (the way you use your hands) and movement around the stage.

For more information, see the Review page opposite. ▷

ⓘ Review

People and places A *stage* is the place where you stand to give a presentation. You use *audience* to talk about the people listening to the *speaker*.
I was so nervous that I couldn't move around the stage.
She was an excellent speaker who inspired the audience.

Getting your message across You use *notes* or *cue cards* (usually just the key words written on small cards) to help you remember the key points of your presentation. You use a *microphone* to make your voice louder, and a *screen* to show text and images. A *slide* is a piece of film with text that can be projected onto a wall or screen.
My notes were quite hard to follow. I'm going to use cue cards next time.
My voice is quite soft so I always use a microphone.
I'm going to show a short video so please look at the screen.

You give a *handout* to your audience. This can be a piece of paper, often with a summary of the main points, or it can be an object, e.g. you product. A *flip chart* has large sheets of paper for writing or drawing on. A *visual aid* is anything your audience can see, e.g. a product, a slide show, a catalogue.
Don't let the audience have the handouts until the end.
He drew some very helpful diagrams on the flip chart.
'What visual aids do you plan to use?'
'A sample of the new product and the promotional poster.'

Technology *PowerPoint* is a computer program. It gives a *slide show* – text and images on a screen. *OHP* stands for overhead projector and *OHT* for overhead transparency. You use the internet to show something as part of a presentation in an *online demo* (*demonstration*).
She gave a PowerPoint presentation but the slide show was too long and complicated.
I'll put the key points on OHTs so that I can display them on the OHP.

The online demo started well but then we lost the internet link.

Stages A *talk* or *presentation* starts with an *introduction* and ends with a *summing up* or a *recap*. Often the audience participates in a *question and answer session*.
Your introduction was too long so you had to rush the recap. There wasn't time for a question and answer session.

Performance It's important to *make eye contact* with your audience and to *project* your voice so everyone can hear you. Your *body language* includes eye contact, *gestures* (the way you use your hands) and moving around the stage.
It's important to make eye contact to involve your audience.
Body language is important – use gestures to emphasize important points, but don't move around too much.
Don't rely on a microphone – learn to project your voice to the back of the room.

EXTRA TIPS

Note that you often use the following phrases in presentations.
Outlining a presentation:
Let me start by
Firstly
Then we'll look at
Finally I'll outline
Referring to a visual aid:
As you can see
Changing topic:
Let's move on to
That brings me to
Recapping:
I'd like to go over
Summarizing:
So, to sum up
Inviting questions:
Does anyone have any questions?

Conferences

Test it ✔

1 Follow the instructions to find words connected with conferences.

Are you willing to give the
opening address on the last day? change four letters _closing_

a We need a **menu** with computer
equipment. change one letter
and add one letter ....

b We're doing a **workroom** on
listening skills. change three letters ....

c There's a plan of the conference
hall in your conference **sack**. change one letter ....

d The **keyhole** speaker is an HR
expert. change two letters ....

e I can't make the **seminal** on the
last day. change one letter ....

f You can get more information
from our company **sand**. add one letter ....

g I'm the **delete** from Tecnik Solutions. add two letters ....

h The sales **confer** starts on 17 July. add four letters ....

i The **facilitate** at the conference
were awful. change three letters ....

j There's coffee and other **refreshers**
on level 2. change two letters
and add two letters ....

k Everyone attended the plenary
lesson. change one letter
and add one letter ....

l We're expecting 100 people to
amend the conference. change one letter
and add one letter ....

2 There's one wrong word in each sentence. Delete the incorrect option.

Where shall we hold/~~make~~/have the conference?

a Are you giving a discourse/speech/talk this year?
b I've just been to a brilliant delegate/seminar/workshop.
c Our company can offer a range of committees/facilities/refreshments.
d There wasn't much opportunity to network/make contacts/exchange contacts.
e All delegates must attend the closing address/plenary session/keynote speaker.
f Please sign up/attend/register for the conference at least a month in advance.

GO to page 84 and check your answers.

Test it again ✔

1 **Choose the correct words to complete the dialogue.**

~~conference~~ address facilities workshop seminars speeches
venue delegates attending speakers talk

KARL Hi there, Emma. How was the ....*conference*.....?
EMMA Not bad, thanks. There were **a** .... **b** .... from all the
national offices, so it was good to meet up with them. The
c .... was a bit strange though. It was an old house in the
country – quite comfortable but very low-tech. They didn't have
d .... for PowerPoint presentations and there was no internet
access in the bedrooms.
KARL How strange. And wasn't there a problem with the **e** ....?
EMMA Yes, the microphone wasn't working so all the **f** .... had to
shout. The head of the Hong Kong office gave the opening
g .... but we could hardly hear her.
KARL You gave a **h** .... too, didn't you?
EMMA Well, it was more of a **i** .... for a small group. It was a practical
session on communication skills. It went quite well, actually. I went to all
the **j** .... on new markets, too. There's so much to learn about
business in other countries.

2 **Find and correct eight mistakes in the sentences.**

I don't think conferences are good places to ~~give~~ new contacts.	...*make*......
a I changed business cards with about twenty other delegates.	....
b Where are we giving the sales conference this year?	....
c We're going to a conference in e-commerce.	....
d A business conference can be a great place to network.	....
e Please register for the conference by 21 March.	....
f I didn't have time to stay for the opening address as I had to get back to the office.	....
g If you go to our stand, you can get samples of our new products.	....
h In my job I assist about ten conferences a year.	....
i The hotel wasn't a very good workshop for the conference.	....
j We were very hungry by lunchtime because no one had ordered any refreshments.	....
k I didn't enjoy the plenary speech. There were just too many people.	....
l The keynote talker was very entertaining.	....
m Please collect your conference packs from the main desk.	....

⚙ Fix it

Answers to Test it
Check your answers. Wrong answer?
Read the right Fix it note to find out why.

1
- • closing → D
- a venue → B
- b workshop → E
- c pack → F
- d keynote → D
- e seminar → E
- f stand → F
- g delegate → C
- h conference → A
- i facilities → B
- j refreshments → B
- k session → E
- l attend → A

2
- • ~~make~~ → A
- a ~~discourse~~ → D
- b ~~delegate~~ → E, C
- c ~~committees~~ → B
- d ~~exchange contacts~~ → G
- e ~~keynote speaker~~ → D, E
- f ~~attend~~ → A

Now go to page 83. Test yourself again.

Answers to Test it again

1
a delegates	f speakers
b attending	g address
c venue	h talk
d facilities	i workshop
e speeches	j seminars

2 The incorrect sentences are:
a ~~changed~~	exchanged
b ~~giving~~	having/holding
c ~~in~~	on
f ~~opening~~	closing
h ~~assist~~	attend
i ~~workshop~~	venue
k ~~speech~~	session
l ~~talker~~	speaker

⚙ Fix it notes

A A *conference* is a large, formal meeting. You *have* or *hold* a conference *on* a particular subject. You *attend* a conference if you go to it. You *register* or *sign up* when you book your place or when you arrive.

B The *venue* is where a conference takes place. Conference *facilities* include rooms, equipment and services. *Refreshments* are small amounts of food and drink.

C A *delegate* is a person at a conference sent to represent others.

D *Speakers* are the people who *give talks/speeches*. A *keynote speaker* gives the most important speech. The *opening address* is given at the start and the *closing address* at the end.

E A *plenary session* is attended by all participants at a conference. A *seminar* is a meeting for giving and discussing information; a *workshop* is a meeting for improving skills by doing practical exercises.

F A *stand* is a table/temporary structure where a company displays information, hands out samples, etc. A *conference pack* is a set of documents giving information about times, places, etc.

G You *make contacts* when you meet new people. You *network* when you talk to other/new people about business opportunities. You often *exchange business cards*.

For more information, see the Review page opposite. ▷

ⓘ Review

Conferences A *conference* is a large, formal meeting for the staff of one organization or for a range of organizations.
There's a conference in Lima on 7 May.

You *have* or *hold* a conference on a particular subject. You *attend* a conference if you go to it. You *register* or *sign up* when you book a place in advance or when you arrive at a conference.
We're having a conference on business in the 21st century.
We're holding this year's conference in July.
We're expecting about 450 people to attend the conference.
I signed up for the conference online.

> **EXTRA TIPS**
> You can use a range of nouns with *conference* to say what the theme is, e.g. *sales conference, trade conference, pharmaceutical conference.*

Places and things The *venue* is where a conference takes place if it isn't at a company's offices. It can be e.g. a hotel, conference centre or business park.
It might be hard to find a venue at such short notice.

Conference *facilities* include rooms for meetings and for people to stay in, computer and technical equipment, and services like meals and transport.
Some of the facilities at the conference were excellent, but the food was awful.

Refreshments are small amounts of food and drink like tea and coffee, water, sandwiches and biscuits.
Refreshments are served in Room 1A.

A *stand* is a table/temporary structure where a company displays information, hands out samples, etc.
If you visit our stand, you can find out more about our services.

A *conference pack* is a set of documents giving information about times, places, etc. It typically includes a map of the venue, list of delegates, timetable of sessions, and local information.
Delegates will be sent a conference pack on receipt of payment.

People A *delegate* is a person at a conference sent to represent others. It's also often used to refer to any person who attends a conference.
How many delegates attended the engineering conference?

Speakers are the people who *give talks/speeches*. A *keynote speaker* gives the most important speech.
All the speakers gave impressive talks.
The keynote speaker summed up the issues discussed at the conference.

Sessions The *opening address* is given at the start and the *closing address* at the end.
The opening address set the tone for the rest of the conference.

A *plenary session* is attended by all participants at a conference.
The plenary session gave delegates the opportunity to give their opinions.

A *seminar* is a meeting for giving and discussing information; a *workshop* is a meeting for improving skills by doing practical exercises.
We discussed a range of techniques in the customer services seminar.
Workshops are limited to a maximum of ten delegates.

Verbs You *make contacts* when you meet new people. You *network* when you talk to other/new people about business opportunities. You often *exchange business cards*.
I really enjoy networking and making new contacts.

British and American English

Differences in grammar

🇬🇧 British English	🇺🇸 American English
Present perfect and past simple	
You use the present perfect to give news.	You can use either the present perfect or the past simple to give news.
The share price has fallen by 50 points.	*The share price fell by 50 points.*
You use the present perfect with *just, already* and *yet.*	You can also use the present perfect or the past simple with *just, already* and *yet.*
I've just found a new job.	*I've just found a new job.* OR *I just found a new job.*
Have you finished the report yet?	*Did you finish the report yet?*
The past participle of *get* is *got.*	The past participle of *get* is *gotten.*
Our performance has got worse.	*Our performance has gotten worse.*
The verbs *burn, dream, lean, leap, learn, smell, spell, spill* and *spoil* can end in *-ed* or *-t* in the past simple and past participle.	In American English, you use the regular *-ed* ending.
We learnt/learned a lot from the experience.	*We learned a lot from the experience.*
Have and have got	
You use *have got* or *have* to talk about possession.	You usually use *have* to talk about possession.
We've got offices in Paris.	*We have offices in Paris.*
Shall and should	
You can use *shall* or *should* to ask for advice.	You usually use *should* to ask for advice.
What shall/should I tell my boss?	*What should I tell my boss?*
Prepositions	
There are differences in the use of prepositions:	
at the weekend	*on the weekend*
Monday to Friday	*Monday through Friday*
stay at home	*stay home*
write to someone	*write someone*
a quarter to six	*a quarter of/to six*
a quarter past eight	*a quarter after eight*
in this street	*on this street*
different from/to	*different from/than*
Collective nouns	
You can use a singular or plural verb with nouns like *government, team, company, staff.*	In American English, you use a singular verb with collective nouns.
The sales team is/are performing well.	*The sales team is performing well.*

Differences in spelling and vocabulary

🇬🇧 British English	🇺🇸 American English

Spelling

Verbs such as *organise/organize*, *prioritise/prioritize* can end -*ise* or -*ize*.	These verbs always end -*ize*.
I'm organising this year's conference.	*I'm organizing this year's conference.*

Other spelling differences include:			
travel	→ *travelling/travelled*	*travel*	→ *traveling/traveled*
cancel	→ *cancelling/cancelled*	*cancel*	→ *canceling/canceled*
-our	→ *colour, labour*	*-or*	→ *color, labor*
-tre	→ *centre, litre*	*-ter*	→ *center, liter*
-nce	→ *defence, pretence*	*-nse*	→ *defense, pretense*
-l-	→ *skilful, instalment*	*-ll-*	→ *skillful, installment*

Vocabulary

aeroplane	airplane
angry	mad
barrister, solicitor	attorney, lawyer
bill	check
chips, crisps	(French) fries, potato chips
clever	smart
dialling code	area code
dustbin	garbage can
engaged (on the phone)	busy
flat	apartment
football	soccer
ground floor, first floor	first floor, second floor
go on holiday	go on vacation
have a bath/shower	take a bath/shower
ill	sick
lift	elevator
litter/rubbish	garbage
main road, motorway	highway, freeway
metro/underground	subway
mobile (phone)	cell phone
pavement	sidewalk
petrol	gasoline (gas)
railway	railroad
return ticket	round trip
rise	raise
single ticket	one-way ticket
sweets	candy
tap	faucet
timetable	schedule
toilet	washroom
windscreen	windshield

Useful information

Dates and phone numbers

In British and American English you write and say dates in different ways:

Writing dates
UK   *12 August* OR *12/8*
US   *August 12* OR *8/12*

Saying dates
UK   *the eleventh of June* OR *June the eleventh*
US   *eleven June* OR *June eleven*

UK   2009   *two thousand and nine*
US   2009   *two thousand nine* OR *two thousand and nine*

Using the phone
UK   *Hello, Peter Merton speaking.*
US   *Hello, this is Peter Merton.*

UK   *'Is that Peter?' 'Yes, speaking.'*
US   *'Is this Peter?' 'Yes, this is Peter.'*

In British and American English, when you give someone a phone number, you pause between sets of numbers.

UK   01608 684108   oh one six oh eight (pause) six eight four one oh eight
US   212-706 6376   two one two (pause) seven oh six (pause) six three seven six
              OR   two one two (pause) seven zero six (pause) six three seven six

British and American money

Britain has not adopted the euro, so it still uses its own money or currency, called pounds sterling. British money is divided into two types: pounds (£) and pence (p). One hundred pence = one pound. There are eight coins: a penny, 2 pence, 5 pence, 10 pence, 20 pence, 50 pence, a pound and 2 pounds. There are four banknotes: £5, £10, £20 and £50.

The United States uses the dollar as its currency. This also is divided into two types: dollars and cents. One hundred cents = one dollar. There are five coins: a penny or a cent, a nickel or 5 cents, a dime or 10 cents, a quarter or 25 cents and a dollar. There are five banknotes: $1, $5, $10, $20, $50.